2 -

The Grand
Experiment

ANOUK RIDE

The Grand Experiment

Two Boys, Two Cultures

HACHETTE AUSTRALIA

HACHETTE AUSTRALIA

Published in Australia and New Zealand in 2007
by Hachette Australia
(An imprint of Hachette Livre Australia Pty Limited)
Level 17, 207 Kent Street, Sydney NSW 2000
Website: www.hachette.com.au

National Library of Australia
Cataloguing-in-Publication data

Ride, Anouk.
   The grand experiment.

   ISBN 978 0 7344 0920 1

   1. Conaci. 2. Dirimera. 3. Salvado, Rosendo, 1814–1900.
   4. Benedictines—Missions—Western Australia—New Norcia—
   History 5. New Norcia (W.A.)—Biography. 6. Children,
   Aboriginal Australian—Western Australia—Neew Norcia—
   Biography. 7. Children, Aboriginal Australian—Italy—Cava—
   Biography. I. Title.

305.8991509412

Edited by Jean Dunn
Cover design by Luke Causby/Blue Cork
Typeset in 12.25/16 Centaur MT by Bookhouse, Sydney
Printed in Australia by Griffin Press, Adelaide

The publisher would like to thank the Benedictine Community of New
Norcia Archive for its kind permission to reproduce extracts from E. J.
Stormon's translation of Rosendo Salvado's memoirs, and other
photographs, engravings and correspondence from the collection.

Cover photographs
Top: The Benedictine monastery of New Norcia in Western Australia
as it stands today. The monastery was established by Spanish missionaries,
Salvado Rosendo and José Serra, in 1849. Soon after, Salvado would
escort two Aboriginal boys to Europe for monastic education. (Courtesy
Lucas Ride)
Bottom: Dirimera (*left*) and Conaci, the two Nyungar boys whom Salvado
Rosendo accompanied to Europe in 1849 to be educated as Benedictine
monks. (Courtesy Benedictine Community of New Norcia Archive)

Hachette Livre Australia's policy is to use papers
that are natural, renewable and recyclable products
and made from wood grown in sustainable forests.
The logging and manufacturing processes are expected
to conform to the environmental regulations
of the country of origin.

Contents

Preface

Every day we see thousands of images—photographs, paintings, billboards, television, films, magazines, newspapers, the list goes on and on. We are surrounded by so many images that we do not have time to record them in our mind's eye let alone remember them. Despite this, some images have the power to change lives and the course of history for ever.

A nineteenth-century drawing of two Aboriginal boys dressed in monastic robes changed my life. I saw it at New Norcia, a stone and brick Spanish monastery built on the flat plains northeast of Perth, surrounded by wheat fields and eucalypts. Tucked away in the museum of New Norcia, the image was scantily labelled and displayed without any sense of importance. The sketch was compelling—a short, chubby-faced cheeky boy and his long-faced serious friend looking straight at me. My curiosity was aroused by their unsmiling stare.

Most children's eyes have a look about them, a look of not knowing everything, of being young. But some children have eyes that are older—you see it in kids who have lived in the streets, you see it in places in the world where life is tough and there is little time for childhood because everyone must fend for themselves. Looking at this image of two Aboriginal boys in New Norcia's museum, I saw it again—the wisdom of suffering in the eyes of children.

I did not even know their names, but I knew I had to know more about these two boys, dressed in dark monastic robes. I knew that this image had an untold significance for Australian history, and somehow for myself. So, I began to do some research about them, the drawing, and how they came to be monks.

That was ten years ago. I lived in Britain and Switzerland and travelled across Europe and Asia. Jobs, people and places came and went, yet the image of those two boys remained with me. When I was in Europe, I talked to monks, visited monasteries and read about religious iconography and religious history. When I lived in Britain, I spent hours in regional and national museums and libraries unearthing documents on colonial history. When I returned to Australia, I listened to stories of Aboriginal people removed from their parents when they were young, learned about Aboriginal art and stories—myths, I was told, that began before the beginning and end long after the end.

Even when I was not researching the story, everywhere I went seemed to remind me of those two boys. From black women on Buka island in Bougainville laughing about how they felt out of place in Beijing, to families arguing in Italian in cafes in Melbourne, people alluded to personal stories of travel, adventure, loss and longing.

Although I have made every effort to ensure that the facts in this story are true, this book is a personal story too. It is my individual interpretation of the voyage of two young Aboriginal boys in a time of guilt, innocence and great naivety in the history of Australia and the world.

This tale is set in the mid-1800s, when large parts of Australia were still undiscovered by white settlers. Australia was seen in Europe as a land of opportunity, but also of harshness. Who knew what would be done about the 'savages' who lived there? Who could tell how long its desert stretched and what it would do to grown men? Who could say what wild animals lived there and what a person would find?

Adventurous Europeans wrote home of a land so different to the soft hills of Britain or the forests of Europe that it was unimaginable to those they had left behind. They wrote letters, diaries and books to record their experiences. But the Aboriginal people they encountered had an oral history and did not set down their stories on paper or in writing. Their individual experiences of what happened when Australia was invaded are now—like many of their tribal customs—lost.

This is part of what makes that drawing of two boys dressed in monastic robes unique. It left behind an impression of what their individual lives were like at a time when the lives of Aboriginal people were, for the most part, considered cheap and expendable. An estimated 20 000 Aboriginal people were killed directly through the violence that followed when Australia was invaded and settled by the British after 1788.[1] Many more tens of thousands died of diseases to which they had not been exposed until the arrival of white settlers.

In the 1840s, when this story is set, Aboriginal people were considered by white settlers as a people to be controlled, managed and civilised—they were rarely listened to and even more seldom understood. However, these two Aboriginal boys left behind letters, and records of conversations and stories told about them, which tell us of their experiences. Here is the story of Conaci and Dirimera—the story that the little sketch alone could not tell me.

⌒

I owe many thanks to others for their help in uncovering the details of Conaci and Dirimera's adventure. This story did not start with a blank page but with significant work on the history of New Norcia and the local Aboriginal tribes who came into contact with the mission. I would like to acknowledge, in particular, the work of George Russo and Antonio Linage Conde in researching the life of Rosendo Salvado, and that of E. J. Stormon in translating Salvado's memoirs into English. Neville Green and Lois Tilbrook, who compiled information on the Nyungar people, Mudrooroo, who has studied Aboriginal beliefs, and the South West Aboriginal Land and Sea Council all shaped my consciousness regarding local and Australian history and gave context to the events that these pages describe.

Many thanks for direct assistance in researching this story must go to the archivists of New Norcia Monastery, Western Australia, and St Paul's Outside the Walls Monastery, Rome, as well as to the staff of the National Library of Australia in Canberra and the Battye Library in Perth. Our understanding of the world is made possible by the untiring work of archivists and librarians like these over the centuries.

For researching and producing the photographs, I am grateful for the help of Lucas Ride. I would also like to thank Silvio di Cocco for introducing me to southern Italy and for his translation and research support for those parts of the story set in Rome and Badia di Cava de' Tirreni. For her good humour and encouragement while I wrote the final pages of this book, I am indebted to Jane Sweeney. For literary advice and support, my thanks will always go to commissioning editor Teresa Pitt and fellow writers Moira Callegari and Susan Borg. Finally, for being my greatest critic and supporter, I would like to thank Heather Ride.

Anouk Ride
Sydney, 2007

Nyungar stories are like the ocean waves
washing up on the beaches.
Every wave changes the coastline and washes up
something new.

Trevor Walley,
great great-grandson of one of the many Nyungar people
who knew Spanish missionary, Rosendo Salvado.[2]

If these events were not factual,
nobody would believe them,
but believe them or not
the truth is that they took place.

Rosendo Salvado,
at the beginning of his memoirs.[3]

Land

The plains around the mission of New Norcia seemed so tranquil, I remember thinking, as I looked out the car window. My parents drove and I was in the back seat, recalling all those hours spent in the car in my youth. We had lived in about ten different houses in four states in Australia, plus two years living in the United States, during the nineteen years I lived with my family. There was no particular reason for all this moving other than a combination of our collective circumstances, opportunities and ambitions. We also took holidays—at least once a year—and between the moving and the holidays, in days before flights became as affordable as they are now, there was a lot of driving. We once worked out that we had driven the distance from the bottom of Australia to the very top during those years.

As a result, drives that to some people seem epic—eight hours or more—do not bother me at all. There is not much to do when you are in a car for that long, except think. As a child, I would look out the window and daydream, making up fantastical stories. Now twenty-two years old, after my first visit to New Norcia mission, I thought about the two Aboriginal boys in the photo and the land that they came from.

When the boys were born, much of this land would have been forested—eucalyptus covering the small hills and growing over rivers that reflected silver light at the sun. Only the long, flat plains would have been open grasslands, providing fodder for kangaroos and wallabies. The expanse of space here would have been endless, as infinite as the blue, open sky. All that would have been seen on the horizon was a shimmer of imaginary water reflecting the heat of the day.

As we drove on paved roads, I thought that if the sky became closer and darker and the eucalypts were replaced with oaks, the land around New Norcia could look like England— at least in the winter, when green. Cleared of many trees and fenced to keep in sheep, the land seemed to have been tamed. The town names on signposts also recalled England: 'Guildford', 'York', 'Avon Valley Park'.

When you are in the middle of the central Australian desert or a northern rainforest, placenames like these—recalling the countries and towns where white settlers were from—can seem silly, an absurd attempt to mark an unfamiliar landscape with something more ordinary. But around New Norcia that day, an area that became known as the Victoria Plains, the land seemed so genteel that such English names were not entirely out of place.

I had to remind myself that this land had not always been like this. This land was once a natural habitat for wild animals, *untouched by farming and foreigners. The only people who had lived here were members of the Yuet tribe, who lived in makeshift camps by the river. When Conaci and Dirimera were infants, white settlers had not surveyed this land and the contest for its ownership was only just beginning.*

In the heat of the day, through sunglasses and a car window, I squinted at a blur of beige and dark green. As members of the Yuet tribe, Conaci and Dirimera would have seen this place very differently. Their people were raised with an understanding and connection to this land that Europeans would at first not understand, then ignore, and much later come to envy.

The dawn murmur of birds in the dark eucalypts was interrupted by the long shout of a man. It was the tribal call of the fight. The people of the Yuet tribe woke quickly, the men firing back spears at their foes, the women gathering the children to run and hide. Dirimera was one boy among them. Just nine years old, he stood up and began running.

It must almost have felt like he was still dreaming when he heard his skin rip. A spear pierced through Dirimera's stomach and came out his back. As family scooped up his body and ran to safety, the men of his tribe shouted and threw more spears to chase out another tribe that was pushing onto their land.

It was just another consequence of the land grab outside Perth, the capital of the newly settled Swan River colony, in the 1840s. The new settlers, many of them former soldiers and naval officers, moved further inland and claimed land for farming at half the price or less of land in their home countries of Britain and Ireland. Fenced out and pushed into closer contact with each other, the tribes fought among themselves for the remnants of land that had not been claimed by settlers. Dirimera's tribe was part of a group of Aboriginal people living in the southeast of Western Australia, known as Nyungar or Nyoongar. His tribe was called Yuet, which means 'No'. When they knew their land was contested, the Yuet tribesmen fought back fiercely.

An old man took charge of carrying Dirimera's limp body, being careful not to move the spear, which everyone knew would increase the loss of blood. There was one place they had heard of where white men had healed several Yuet people—a woman was cured of sores, a man's ears were unblocked, another man's stomach pain was removed. Dirimera's family took him directly to the white man's place of healing: a mission built in the bush by European missionaries.

Unlike farmers, the monks did not chase Aboriginal people off their land, and so the Yuet people had not resisted the newcomers and some had even helped build the mission—a small chapel, a few whitewashed huts and a vegetable garden. Dirimera's mother, Callango, knew the settlement well and led the others up the slope.

The solemn tones of the Benedictine monks reciting their morning service echoed out of the small stone building in the bush. Callango reached the mission first and called out that her son was hurt. The stocky Spaniard, Rosendo Salvado, went to the door to meet her and to see what was the cause of the commotion.

A white-haired man, most probably Dirimera's grand-father, carried the boy to Salvado. Dirimera's serious brows were furrowed in deep pain, his long face was frighteningly pale and his eyes opened and closed as he moved in and out of consciousness. The spear's tear was wide and, according to Salvado, 'the wound was so bad that the only thing we could do was prepare him for death'.[1]

Salvado lay Dirimera down on a bed in one of the mission's huts. He slowly removed the spear. Blood soaked the white sheets and Salvado's fingers. Dirimera probably knew that losing this much blood was dangerous and that death was close. He could hear his mother weeping and wailing outside the hut with the rest of the family as they waited anxiously. The monks did not want to admit to Dirimera's family that their curative powers were largely due to luck rather than any medical knowledge—their only medical supplies were digestive salts and laxatives.

Another Spanish monk, the short and humourless José Serra, cleansed the wound with what they thought was the most suitable substance: olive oil. Then Salvado stitched the circular wound with a thick needle and thread, smiling a desperate grimace at the frightened boy, until the hole in Dirimera's stomach had closed. Salvado then lathered the area in olive oil and changed the bloody bedding. Salvado and Serra held Dirimera's head and made him swallow a cup of sugary tea and a laxative, and then left him to sleep. His family sneaked into the hut to see the boy, who was looking pale, pained and spent as he took shallow breaths in his slumber.

Bed-bound and weak, Dirimera stayed in the hut for several days. He had never been in a solid building before. Now he lay on clean white sheets and looked at white-washed walls. He was fed rice soup and tea and cleansed with olive oil by white men whom he came to know by name. From Galicia, in northern Spain, a region known for its fervour, fishing and dry humour, was the monk Salvado. He liked to laugh and sing, impressing Indigenous and non-Indigenous people alike with his optimism and vitality. From southern Spain, the Catalan monk Serra was more proud and sombre—a hardworking and strict man, he had a tendency to alienate those who did not share his beliefs. When Aboriginal people seeing white men for the first time pulled on Salvado's beard, he laughed; when they did this to Serra, he became furious. Salvado liked to go out exploring, hunting and travelling in the bush, whereas Serra hid his fear of animals and the wild by attending to the mission buildings and garden.

Dirimera called Serra 'Kiara' because the sound of 'Serra' was too foreign to his tongue. He thanked him for the medicine, but it was Salvado who would have smiled at Dirimera when he winced in pain.

Since Salvado had arrived in Australia in January 1846, he had written down every Nyungar word he heard. He soon learned to double-check them, after the time he asked a man for the name for water and one of them told him, '*cona*'. He later found out that '*cona*' meant 'shit'. However, his keen ear and his discipline in writing down what he heard meant he had learned a little of the local Yuet language in the few months before Dirimera arrived. So, it was Salvado who talked to and soothed Dirimera's parents about their youngest son's perilous condition.

At the door to the hut, Dirimera's eleven-year-old brother and his mother waited with several other Yuet women for news. Setting up camp there, they drew on their own resources to try and restore Dirimera to health. They cried and sang songs to him during the day. At night they lay huddled together on the ground, covered themselves with kangaroo skins and slept, keeping spiritual watch over Dirimera from outside the white walls.

One of the beliefs of the Yuet tribe was that a life taken or saved was owed a life in return. If a man saved a boy, then that boy and his family owed the man a life. So, more than just 'an eye for an eye', it was a way of expressing appreciation and loyalty. One man who had a number of ulcers was treated at the mission and became well. He tried to thank Salvado, who wrote, 'Not knowing any other way of expressing his gratitude, he burst out with this, "When you die, I will be so sorry that I will kill six natives, not just one, so that everyone will see how much I think of you".' Most Yuet people who were cured at the mission said that they would trade their lives or someone else's in gratitude.[2] Instead, Salvado convinced such people to work at the mission on tasks such as constructing huts, tending its gardens, clearing land or building what is now called Brothers' Road (which can still be seen to the left of Geraldton Road at Hay Flat).[3]

It seemed like a miracle when, after nine days of rest, tea, rice and continual application of olive oil to the wound, Dirimera stood up and walked outside the hut. Callango took her son in her arms. When Salvado came over to the family, Dirimera's father, Nalbinga, told the Spanish monk, 'Our son is your son, our daughters are your daughters'.[4]

Dirimera did not go back with his family to live with the other Yuet people. Salvado and his parents decided that he would instead stay on the mission. Dirimera was young, but the primary value that was instilled in Yuet children was respect for their elders. So on presentation of this news, Dirimera was seemingly neither happy nor sad but accepting of a fate that, thanks to his extraordinary recovery, was no longer his to choose. Salvado, on the other hand, was excited as he now had an Aboriginal recruit to fulfil his heart's desire: Christianising the local Yuet people.

⌒

Salvado's religious fervour was born in his early life experiences. Born on 1 March 1814, he came from a region where stubbornness was considered a great virtue. The Spanish town where he was born, Tuy, overlooked the Portuguese border and was known for being one of only a few that had successfully resisted the invasion of the Moors and Islam in the eighth-century religious wars that had ruptured Spain. When Salvado was a teenager, in the 1830s, the Catholic Church was under attack. Liberals and nationalists instigated uprisings in Spain, France and Italy as a new idea, democracy, began to gather momentum and to challenge the power of European aristocracies.

When he was fifteen years old, Salvado entered the Benedictine monastery of Saint Martin de Compostela in a Spanish city that was known as the third most holy site after Jerusalem and Rome. Even today, thousands still walk the traditional pilgrimage, wearing the scallop shell, to this place—Santiago de Compostela in Galicia—to see the place where many believe a hermit was led by a bright star to the corpse of Saint James.[5] In this city, Salvado met the older José Serra, an orphan who could remember nothing but life at the monastery. Serra, who would come to be Salvado's mentor and co-founder of New Norcia mission on the other side of the world, thought the democracy movement scandalous and a dire threat to the power of the Catholic Church.

The government and the middle class had their eyes on Church wealth, which they sought to unlock. In the anti-religious furore sweeping Spain, almost all churches and monasteries, including those in Galicia, were closed. Monks and those training to be monks were suddenly homeless. Salvado and Serra were turned out on the street.

Salvado went home to live with his parents until he decided what to do next. He became interested in a girl, and worked as a music teacher.[6] Serra had no such distractions—he made his way directly to Italy, where around Rome the Church still held control. Thanks to Serra's persistent lobbying of Church leaders, Salvado was offered a place in the monastery of Badia di Cava de' Terreni in southern Italy. The monasteries in Italy over-flowed with monks who had been forced out of their retreats in their own countries in similar circumstances to Salvado's. It was at Badia di Cava de' Terreni monastery that Salvado and Serra decided to embark together on a journey to Australia, where ultimately they would Christianise unknown Aboriginal tribes.[7]

Once in the Australian bush, Father Salvado and Father Serra found that Christianising the local Yuet people was not easy. The people spent their days gathering bush fruit and seeds or hunting, and there was scarce time to devote to learning about Christianity—even if they had the inclination to do so. Salvado initially tried to talk to Yuet people during the hunt, learning quickly that this was useless when their concentration was on the quest for food. He noted:

> When they are back from the hunt and are sitting around their fire the right moment comes, for then their minds are free and they busy themselves simply with getting food ready, putting their weapons in order or repeating their legends and stories as the Arabs do.[8]

At such times, Salvado found some pretext for joining them:

> When the opportunity offered, we would question the narrator, or even contradict him to draw him out; he on his side would heatedly insist that what he said was true and continue with his story. At other times we would cast some doubt on some details or else let him know that he was contradicting other natives.[9]

It is clear that the elders were protective of their beliefs. When Salvado pushed for answers or challenged some of their beliefs they dismissed him with comments such as, 'You know nothing about it' or, 'You can not understand'.

In many parts of Western Australia the word used by Nyungar tribes to describe Europeans was '*djanga*'—the same word as was used for the spirits of the dead. There does not seem to be evidence that this was a belief for Yuet people, but they recognised that the monks were not part of the spiritual life they knew. They used this different status of the monks to their advantage. For example, they feared a giant serpent they called Uocol, which lived in a waterhole and guarded his lair from greedy Yuets. But they developed the practice of making Salvado approach the waterhole and of following in single file behind his back. This way Uocol could not see them and would see Salvado as the intruder. Despite Salvado's arguments that this belief was 'superstition', the Yuets convinced him to help them disguise themselves from Uocol and were pleased that in this way they could use another source of fresh water.[10]

Yuet people also used Salvado's interest in preaching to obtain help and supplies. They traded their attention for food, leading Salvado to write:

> It is not hard to preach to a native, but it does not do much good, for he will interrupt the missionary and say: 'Everything you tell me may well be quite true; but I am hungry—are you going to give me some bread or not?' If you do not give him some, he will turn his back on you and go off into the bush to find something to eat.[11]

Even after living with the Yuet people for a year, Salvado, Serra and the other monks (French Brother, Leandre Fontienne, and Irish novice, John Gorman) had not secured any interest from the adults in Christianity, let alone conversions. But Salvado had gathered a group of Yuet children, who were left in his care during the day while their parents attended to hunting and other business.

In many parts of Spain, tradition dictated that one child in the family (usually the youngest) would be earmarked for the priesthood. Salvado and Serra noted that the quick minds of the young Yuets would make them suitable to schooling, and that the natural musical abilities of Yuet people would be well suited to Mass and other Catholic ceremonies.

Partly out of tradition, and partly out of necessity, they ceased trying to convert adults and turned their attention to the children. They came to the conclusion that the only way a Yuet was going to understand and embrace the Christian faith was if they heard it from another Yuet. The children were the key, and Salvado decided that it was they who must be schooled as missionaries—an undertaking he would now refer to as 'the grand experiment'.

The small cluster of children who came to live on the mission were largely those whom their parents had pledged in gratitude, like Dirimera, or children who had been orphaned. But one of the children who joined the monks, seemingly without persuasion or coercion, was a cherub-faced seven-year-old boy called Conaci, who came to be Dirimera's dearest friend.

When Conaci was born his father saw a black cockatoo fly by and, in celebration of its spirit, named the boy after the bird. Like his namesake, Conaci was cheeky, loud and sociable, in contrast to the quieter, calmer Dirimera. An opportunist, Conaci is likely to have joined the monks out of curiosity. He was highly intelligent and would have been quick to make himself useful to the monks by telling them stories about Yuet culture and picking up language for communication between the Spaniards and his own community. Conaci learned and told many stories about the mission and the monks' abilities to other Yuets and visiting tribes. The most famous of these stories became 'The Lady Who Knows So Much'—otherwise known as 'Mary, Mother of God'.

Today at New Norcia a shrine stands in the place where Mary is said to have intervened in the lives of men—the Marian Shrine. The story goes that the monks were reaping when they saw a burning bush close to their pile of cut wheat. They attempted to stop the fire from spreading by beating the ground with green branches, but the fire continued to move forward. One of the monks ran into the church and took a painting of the Virgin Mary, given to the monks by Saint Vincent Palotti, from the altar. The Virgin was taken to the corner of the fields nearest the flames and leant against wheat stalks. A few moments later the wind changed direction and the fire was pushed back, saving the valuable crop of wheat. Yuets who saw said, '*Jaco Uilar tenga cumbar! Baal penin, kya baal mekan n-alla tonga but*' (This white lady knows so much! It was she who did it, yes it was she! We can't do things like that.). Conaci was permitted to take his people to the church and show them the Lady Who Knows So Much, and Salvado wrote, 'We were happy enough about this, as it gave us a chance to instruct them in the mysteries of our Faith.'[12]

In the spring of 1847, under the wing of Salvado, Conaci and Dirimera were slowly introduced to European ways and to Christianity. However, Serra too had a protégé—a boy called Upumera—and the beginnings of the competition that would eventually put a rift between Serra and Salvado were being played out through their boys. For in the Australian bush, Salvado saw Serra, who was once his mentor and teacher, in a different light, and came to know his fears and his weaknesses. Salvado's respect for the older monk began to wane.

Tensions within the group of monks were added to by a death at the mission. As the year 1847 began, the monks moved their mission to a new site to escape the memories of the death of the Irish novice, John Gorman. When loading a gun, Brother Fontienne had accidentally fired a shot that killed Gorman almost instantly. A witty and artistic Frenchman, Fontienne had a nervous breakdown as a result of the shooting and had to leave the mission.[13] As an alternate site, the Yuets suggested a pool known as

Mourin, where the monks marked out twenty acres promised by the Western Australian Governor, John Hutt. George Moore, a local farmer, had come across a river the local Yuets called Maura, which was later called Moore River after its 'discoverer'. It was by this river that the mission site was founded.

On 2 January, Salvado began work on a hut at the new site, while Serra went with his boy Upumera to Perth to have the land claim ratified. When the land was formally granted on 1 March 1847, the monks named it after Nursia, the place where the founder of their order, Saint Benedict, had been born. For evermore the Yuet people would live in a place called New Norcia.

Nine months after the founding of the mission, the Benedictine College of New Norcia was opened, and the seven-year-olds Upumera and Conaci, plus the nine-year-old Dirimera, became the first Aboriginal students to attend. Salvado wrote:

> December 8 1847, the feast of the Immaculate Conception, will be remembered by the Australian natives as an auspicious date, because on that day, and under that patronage, the College of New Norcia was opened for their sons. As the first fruits of heaven's blessing, three boys were admitted there and then. These had left their families of their own free will, and with their consent stayed with us henceforth; and soon others followed their example. What a joy it was to see our Mass served by lads who a short time before

were in the night of paganism, and who fled from the white man as if he were a wild beast![14]

To celebrate the opening of the school, the local Yuet people were each given two bowls of soup rather than the customary one bowl.[15]

⌒

Salvado's 'grand experiment' had begun with the three Yuet boys: Upumera, Conaci and Dirimera. Their first lesson was the English alphabet, and already Conaci's keen intellect came to the fore. As Salvado boasted, he learned forty capital and lower-case letters within fifteen minutes and was able to identify and repeat them quickly:

> If the same experiment were conducted in the most highly thought of school in Europe, I wonder if a boy of nine would learn forty letters in ten minutes, have them all off by heart and be able to repeat their names backwards and forwards'.[16]

Conaci's quick learning was especially marked given the different system of counting used by local Yuets: to express multitudes they used the words 'chegyn' (one), 'guggial' (two), 'mau' (three) and 'bulla' (many, or a lot).

The boys' routine at the mission school was to rise at sunrise, and wash and dress to attend Mass and sing hymns. They then had breakfast at seven, completed chores until eight, did light building and farm work for the next three hours, rested at eleven, and ate a piece of bread and played till lunch. School lessons were from two until four or five o'clock, and in the evenings Salvado often played music for them and sang songs. It was very different from the daily life before they went to the mission, when days were spent following their parents as they gathered food or playing amongst themselves.

Salvado noted that he thought Aboriginal children in their own communities were not directed or disciplined by their parents, and thought the children in his care were lucky.[17] He described the boys at the mission as 'excellent and well-behaved lads whose parents were proud of them'. He observed that the college, where boys slept at night and studied during the day, became prestigious for the Yuet people:

Other natives were offended because I had taken some boys into the Mission-house but not theirs, and I had hard work in persuading them that there was only a restricted space and that they could not all fit in. This was clear evidence of heaven's blessing! Before these natives would not have handed their children over to anyone for all the gold in the world, and now they were not merely offering them to us, but were disappointed we did not have room for them all.[18]

In Salvado's vision, the boys would become model citizens—trained in European languages, culture and religion, they would prove to those from the Old World that the Aboriginal people were more than 'savages'. He supposed this demonstration would have the twin outcomes of breaking down apathy and prejudice against Aboriginal people while drawing foreign financiers and supporters to the New Norcia mission. The end result of Salvado's 'grand experiment' would be to bring the boys back from Europe after they had trained and become monks. They would then preach Christianity to their own people.

The 'grand experiment' began with the youngest boy in care of the missionaries, Upumera. He was the first to be baptised, and was renamed Benedict. In the *Inquirer* of 23 February 1848, Salvado reported the plan to the people of Western Australia:

> Benedict Upumera is to remain in Europe for such a period of years as will complete his education in every branch of literature, science and art and then bring him back to this colony when the grand experiment of the civilisation of the Aborigines will be fairly tried on a scale that has never yet been attempted in this part of the world.

Benedict was a privileged boy, wrote Salvado:

> Such was the trust that they reposed in us that, when the news went around that a missionary was leaving for Europe,

the boys argued among themselves who had first choice of going with him on the long journey and the parents showed themselves very happy when it was their boy who was chosen. If it had been otherwise, we would certainly not have been able to take boys to Europe as in fact we did.[19]

Salvado was left behind at New Norcia mission when Serra and Upumera (Benedict) went to Perth in early 1848. While there, Serra was called by Bishop John Brady to go to Europe on business. Salvado wrote:

When he [Upumera] heard that Father Serra was about to leave for the Old World, he asked me to arrange with the Bishop to let him go too. Benedict's father, who was also in Perth, backed up his son's request and the Bishop kindly consented, being confident that Divine Providence meant this boy for its own exalted purpose.[20]

Once tickets for the voyage by ship were booked, Salvado hurried to Perth to say farewell before Serra and Upumera left for Europe:

Although I rode fast day and night, they had already gone to Fremantle when I arrived. I immediately took a fresh horse and galloped towards Fremantle, but while still two miles away I looked out to sea and saw their ship, the *Merope*, which had sailed off ten minutes before, now proudly cutting the waves on its way to Europe. It is easy to understand how bitter a disappointment it was for me to miss saying goodbye to a loved companion and this boy to whom I was so attached. But such was the disposition of God, and I resigned myself to His divine will. I tied my horse to a tree, mounted the top of a hill, and went down on my knees to ask the Lord to protect that fragile ship and bring it safely to port.[21]

This hurried departure was to be an ill omen for Upumera's voyage. Although his willingness and intelligence fostered great hopes for the grand experiment, they were to be quickly dashed.

That winter, Salvado worked to build more huts to house the hoped-for extra missionaries whom Serra was to bring back from Europe. One morning his building work was interrupted by a group of irate Yuets. Leading the group was Upumera's father, Tacancut, a man who had travelled in Western Australia and was accustomed to dealing with white settlers. He asked Salvado angrily whether it was true that Upumera had died on the ship and been thrown into the sea. Salvado said he had heard no such news. Tacancut asked what the 'talking papers' (letters) said on the subject and Salvado assured him that nothing had been written about it. After hearing this news, Upumera's father, according to Salvado, 'seemed calmer and stretched himself on the ground saying, "After all, it would not be any great wonder. Just as he could have died here, he could have died on the ship. But I am quite sure that Father Serra was his very good friend".[22]

But the premonition, suspicion or rumour that led Upumera's father to fear for his son's safety turned out to be right. Although records are vague, it seems Upumera became very ill on that sea voyage from causes unknown. It could have been a common illness, which so often proved fatal to Aboriginal people without previous contact with the West, that killed him. Whatever the cause of his death, when he was only seven years old, the tragedy would not deter the monks from their pursuit of black missionaries in Australia. Instead, unaware of Upumera's death, Salvado turned his energies to his own charges, Conaci and Dirimera.

⌐

When the Benedictines had arrived to establish their mission in 1846, the first words a Yuet man said to Salvado were translated as 'We welcome you to pass here'. Two years later, Conaci and Dirimera were amazed to learn how to transform the land as they helped Salvado farm and construct the mission settlement, which was well established by the end of 1847. [23]

The Yuet people had not farmed but had harvested the land. They dug for a root called 'warran', a potato-like tuber, and left pock marks that would later ensnare the hooves of horses and livestock. The warran was seasonal, as a local farmer James Drummond wrote to the *Inquirer* in May 1842, 'The native yam, called *wyrang* by the natives, the finest esculent vegetable the colony naturally produces, is now beginning to flower'. Drummond noted that the best farming ground was also key land for Nyungars harvesting *warran*: 'When roasted it is represented as superior to the potato, sweet, pleasant and nourishing food. This root flourishes where the best feed for stock is found. Hence the usurpation of the ground and the secret destruction of the Aborigines.'[24]

Salvado and Serra took to farming Yuet land with a devotion equal to their religious passion. The Rule of Saint Benedict, which Salvado and Serra lived their lives by, is largely about creating strong, pious communities with the characteristics of restraint and hard work. Evidence of this latter virtue is found across much of Europe. Monks reclaimed waste land and wetland for agriculture. They opened up lands that otherwise would have remained untouched and they improved tillage, often to the envy of local farmers. Abroad, the clearing of land and building of roads in California, for example, were often done by Benedictine monks in the eighteenth century. Today, many Californian churches and names of settlements can be traced back to the arrival of Spanish missionaries.

At the Italian monastery of Badia di Cava de' Tirreni, Serra and Salvado had been nicknamed 'the two Spanish lemons' for their strength and vitality.[25] Now in Australia, the two men found agricultural life harder than they had imagined. After arriving on the Victoria Plains, Father Serra wrote to Bishop Brady, 'Rosendo reminds me to request Your Excellence to send the boxes of books as soon as possible, because some of them deal with agriculture and without them we will not be able to do anything'. But the Spanish lemons had vigour and they used it to clear nearly 14 hectares of bush on their own. They then ploughed and planted, as Salvado described:

> Father Serra drove the bullocks while I managed the plough. To make the furrows deeper one had to push on the ploughshare with one's feet and these were badly cut by rocks and roots. So we ploughed that land not only with sweat but with blood.[26]

They grew wheat and had nearly 300 metres of vines; there were fig, lemon and olive trees plus potatoes, radishes, tomatoes, parsnips and cucumbers. They could thus feed visiting Yuets on a more regular basis, and as a result many lived nearby.

This abundance stood in contrast to the dwindling stocks of kangaroo faced by the Yuet. Survival in the traditional way was getting harder, while at the mission the living was easy. Shortly after Conaci and Dirimera joined the monks, a flock of 710 sheep arrived at the mission. Salvado recalled that the local people were astonished to see such a large group of these foreign animals. While in surrounding areas, many Aboriginal people killed sheep for food, at the mission the flock was left alone. Salvado trained some Yuet men as shepherds, and so began a gradual transformation from hunter-gatherers to farmhands. Dirimera's younger brother was given the name Andreas and went to work on the mission tending sheep.

Salvado and Serra grazed their stock on 18 000 acres, which they had secured by lease thanks to Salvado's keen business sense. Salvado was the first at the Land Survey Office to purchase land at expiry of local leases. He did detailed surveys of the plains based on Yuet knowledge, he updated government records and he was responsible for many Yuet placenames becoming official and so surviving to this day. Salvado wrote, 'Every time I took up land, I always took care to give the native name of the starting point, well, spring, or even of a marked tree'.[27]

Salvado was a master of letters and contracts, and joked about the Yuets' awe and reverence for the 'talking papers'. They did not understand how an object could communicate. Meanwhile, the 'talking papers' were to establish the missionaries not as passers-by but as owners of the land.

The monks had become a halfway point for Nyungar people between exclusion from land and the freedom they enjoyed before colonisation of Western Australia. White settlers around Perth bought land, fenced it and patrolled borders to keep Nyungar people out. Further inland, particularly in the desert regions of Western Australia,

Aboriginal people were still able to live in their communities in the traditional way. At the mission, Yuet people could live on their land, but this was now owned by the monks who sought to change their behaviour. Some Yuet people became farmhands and helpers at the mission, while others—mostly the elders—continued to live away from the mission but increasingly relied on mission supplies rather than hunting for food.

In this border territory between the West and the traditional, Conaci and Dirimera were encouraged by their parents to learn from the monks. Such was the level of trust between their families and the monks that they allowed the boys to go with Salvado to Perth in December 1848.

The boys climbed up the wooden steps of the bullock wagon. Loaded with wool, it smelt of lanolin and swayed uneasily as Salvado climbed aboard and took the reins. Bishop Brady had ordered Salvado to bring the mission's wool to Perth, so that its sale could bolster the flagging and mismanaged finances of the Western Australian Catholic Diocese. Salvado was put out by the thought that they might not be home on the mission for Christmas, but had to oblige the bishop's wishes by making the trek into the city.

Conaci and Dirimera's first journey took two days. They questioned Salvado about the bullocks and about why they obeyed him. Each took turns at navigating the wagon, amazed at what they could make the bullocks do with just a flick of the reins. They saw other farms for the first time, most of the people waving at Salvado, others looking guarded or hostile. The success of the mission's farming had not been well received by shepherds in particular, who resented the fact that employment and land were being used to the benefit of Nyungar people rather than for their own profit.

When they stopped to rest or make camp at night, the boys stayed close to Salvado. They were well aware that if they wandered on their own without the now well-known 'talking paper', a letter from Salvado explaining the purpose of Yuets straying outside their land, and the words 'Nagna Priest maja Janar' ('I belong to the priest's house') they would be questioned by local tribes and possibly killed as intruders into their territory. Also, local white authorities could have harassed the boys for trespassing.

As the bullock wagon approached Perth, Conaci and Dirimera stared at what was to them an immense settlement. On the banks of the winding Swan River, the settlers of Perth were farming more than 2800 hectares. The land was dotted with thousands of horses, tens of thousands of cattle, hundreds of thousands of sheep and a few pigs and goats. The whitewashed and grey stone buildings gleamed in the sun, while the town's hall and other buildings were twice or three times the size of anything the boys had seen at the mission.

As they entered the streets of Perth, white settlers stared at the bearded monk and his two Aboriginal protégées. Conaci and Dirimera had changed. Their hair, which used to be plastered with animal fat against their heads, was now washed, combed straight and cut. Their skin was smooth—without the horizontal lines of tattoos that were found on the arms and chests of other children— and clean, as they had abandoned the traditional practice of oiling their skin with animal fat. Before coming to the mission, they were naked except for a belt or loincloth; now they dressed in trousers and a shirt, like white boys of their age. They surprised people with their self-assured appearance and their ability to speak a few words of English.

Dirimera and Conaci stared back at the great variety of people in Perth. Seeing white women for the first time, they were amazed at the different colours of hair and skin and by their clothes. By this stage the population of Perth was 4622 people (it had risen from just 1928 in 1838), including 337 Catholics, 3063 Anglicans, 276 Methodists, 187 Independents and 759 Chinese and others. As Salvado put it, on seeing Perth, 'everything made the boys gape in surprise'.[28]

Their astonishment was amusing to Salvado, who had previously been disappointed by the unassuming and bare streets of Perth. Compared to the grandiose churches of Spain's Santiago de Compostela and Italy's monastery at Badia di Cava de' Tirreni, Perth's Catholic church looked threadbare. It had four small bare walls, a half-finished roof, no door and windows. A wooden counter donated by a retired shopkeeper was used as a makeshift altar.[29] On first seeing it, Salvado, so as not to be heard by the assembled mostly Irish and British Catholics, remarked in Latin to Fontienne that if he came inside he could see the world's smallest organ. Nevertheless, the church was a great gain for the minority Catholics of Perth, who were frequently ostracised by the Protestants.

Salvado had previously held a musical concert in Perth, which was remarkable in that he had been able to draw on the support of Jews and Protestants to boost funds raised by his own church for a Catholic mission. The governor of the colony, Andrew Clarke, lent Salvado a large hall in the court house, a Protestant publisher agreed to print programs and posters at his own expense in order to fill the hall, an Anglican minister sent chandeliers from his church to light it and Mr Samson, a local Jewish businessman, sent out invitations and tickets. The piano was borrowed from the Catholic Sisters of Mercy from Dublin, who had established a school in Perth.[30] Salvado's ragged appearance attracted such sympathy that at the end of the concert an old Irish lady insisted on giving him her shoes. She went home barefoot.

An attendance of about sixty people enabled Salvado to raise £70—enough money to buy food, a pair of bullocks and other supplies. The concert included vocal compositions and pieces from opera, Spanish songs and an Aboriginal dance. Salvado was a well-trained and accomplished organist, and the *Perth Gazette* proclaimed on 22 May 1848, the day after the concert:

> His fingers produced sounds that we would have thought were impossible for any instrument to produce. Therefore it is certainly a pity that Mr. Salvado is resigned to a life in the forest, where his eminent talents will be lost. It is a great loss for our white population.

That the population of Perth was hungry for culture was no surprise to Salvado, who thought the place lacking in charm:

> There was very little of interest in the buildings or their layout. One could say that the town was still half-bush for a lot of the original trees were still there in the streets and squares and by the houses, many of which are shaded from the sun by thick-leafed eucalyptus.[31]

About the people of Perth he was more optimistic, noting the excited reception the monks were given and the seeming thirst of the locals for European civilisation. He recorded in his memoirs:

> From the beginning this settlement was made up of people of a much better type than those of the other colonies, where the convicts formed a significant proportion ... There

is no immorality in the Colony, apart from the abuse of alcoholic liquors, and offenses are few and far between, and none very serious. In 1847 a hanging took place which is something extraordinary here. The man sentenced had recently come from another colony, and admitted that he had been corrupted by the example of convicts there.[32]

While the city and its people amazed Conaci and Dirimera, one thing stood out as particularly fascinating for them—a boat. Conaci supposed it was a large fish or animal that could walk on water. Then he saw a ship and asked Salvado, 'Do boats grow into ships when they are older?' Try as they might, Salvado recalled, the Yuet boys could not believe these ships and boats in the distance were not living breathing animals:

We could not manage to convince them that this animal was guided by the rear, for horses, they insisted, have the bit in their mouth and not in their tails (they thought the ropes attached to the rudder were reins) ... Poor lads, everything was new to them! [33]

Little did the boys know that they were soon to set foot on one of these 'animals', otherwise known as a ship.

After spending Christmas in Perth, with a morning Mass at the modest Catholic church, Salvado was ready to go back to the mission. However, Bishop Brady had other plans. When a ship arrived from Sydney on its way to Europe, Brady saw an opportunity to raise funds for his Western Australian diocese: Salvado would go to Europe to spread the news about the successful Central mission.

The other missions under Brady's charge had been failures. The Southern mission—consisting of Father Thébeaux as Superior, Father Tiersé, Vincent N. and Théodore Odon—had left Brady on 6 February 1847 and set out towards Albany on foot. By the end of March they reached Albany but had no source of supplies and were unable to find food in the bush. They became ill, lost a dangerous amount of weight and had to abandon the mission. Instead, the group went to the island of Mauritius, where they worked with the missions of Bishop William Collier.

The Northern mission—comprising Father Angelo Confalonieri as Superior, James Fagan and Nicholas Hogan—boarded a ship leaving Fremantle for Sydney on 1 March 1847. They transferred to another ship sailing to Port Victoria (now known as Darwin) but became shipwrecked in the Torres Strait. Fagan and Hogan, both swimmers, drowned while Confalonieri, who could not swim, managed to survive. Confalonieri reached Port Victoria and attempted conversion of the local Aboriginal people, but died on 9 June 1848 before much progress towards a mission could be made.[34]

The flourishing mission of New Norcia would make Rome forget all this and would open up the purses of churchgoers, Bishop Brady supposed. On 28 December 1848, Brady ordered Salvado to make his way to Rome and told him he was to leave in just nine days. Responsible for the ordination of an Irish catechist, Timothy Donovan, Salvado had no time to go back to New Norcia before the ship departed. As for Conaci and Dirimera, they had no desire to travel back to the mission without Salvado's protection. The month-long stay in Perth had peaked the curiosity of Conaci, while Dirimera had his lifelong debt to pay to Salvado for saving his life.

Salvado secured permission from Brady to take the boys with him to Europe, and wrote in his memoirs that their parents' permission was sought and gained. But how much Conaci's father, Malanga, in particular, understood of the monk's request to take his son is unknown, and likely to have been less than Dirimera's father's comprehension of consent. For Malanga had little contact with the mission or with European settlers.[35]

In contrast, Dirimera's parents—his father, Henry Nalbinga (Nalbinga being his first name until he was given the white name of Henry), and his mother, known as Callango—had both come to live on the mission, and Henry worked on the mission's farm with his other son, Andreas. As numbers of helpers around the mission swelled, Salvado gave his workers a weekly wage. He taught men like Henry to deposit their wages with him in small boxes, keys to which Salvado kept. The wages were undoubtedly low, but the region's common practice was to employ Aboriginal people without pay, the usual justification being that they could not understand the concept of money.

So, since there is nothing in writing to confirm the permission of Conaci and Dirimera's parents, and since it is likely that Serra, with his limited grasp of Yuet language, made the request of the parents, how much was explained to them is unclear.

Meanwhile, in Perth, the boys acquired new guardians. On 6 January 1849 they were baptised by Bishop Brady, who confirmed the names Salvado had given them on the mission. Conaci's wide brow was sprinkled with holy water and he became Francis Xavier Conaci. Dirimera's face remained stern as he was solemnly baptised John Baptist Dirimera.

The Secretary of the Colony, Dr R. R. Madden, and his wife attended the ceremony and officially became the boys' godparents. Madden was the first Catholic leader in Western Australian colonial politics and was eager to bridge the social and political gap between the Catholics and the Anglicans. An Irish surgeon and anti-slavery campaigner, he took a personal interest in the boys, questioning them on their studies and their upcoming trip.[36] He was curious about the idea of 'the grand experiment', supposing that education and civilisation of Aboriginal people might alleviate the racial conflict that, along with the question of whether or not to import convicts, had been controversial throughout his governance. Madden smoothed the way for Salvado, Conaci and Dirimera to travel to Europe, along with himself, his wife and his son Thomas. As part of this esteemed party, the boys were elevated to minor celebrities and attracted cheers as they left Perth to make their way to a ship bound for Great Britain.

Sea

Parents spend much of their time trying to instil in their children the idea that their actions have lasting consequences. It is not an easy task. For instance, most children know that if they do something wrong there will be anger but this will pass, usually after an apology or a show of affection. The idea that the consequences of what they have done wrong could stretch beyond such a rapprochement is not understood. There is always the possibility in a young mind that a child can 'go back' to a place they have been, and have another of the thing they've just had, or that 'dead' doesn't really mean we will not see it any more. The idea of consequences challenges a child's own ego by suggesting that there are things they cannot control. The concept of forever can only be acquired when they get older.

I do not think Conaci understood what he was doing in agreeing to travel overseas with Salvado. How could someone who had always lived in the same place understand what other places *would be like, how far they were from what he knew, how long it would take to travel there and how he would have to change to survive? Salvado's encouragement of Conaci played to the classic vulnerabilities of children: ego and curiosity. Salvado fuelled Conaci's ego—telling the boy he was especially bright and had been chosen to be one of the first Aboriginal people to become a monk. Then, of course, Conaci followed his curiosity and, like many children, conveniently put aside any thought of the consequences.*

Dirimera was different—his scarred stomach was a constant reminder of the concept of forever. The path of his life had been set, as are the lives of brides in arranged marriages or of indentured servants. Dirimera's debt to Salvado and Serra for saving him from death meant that he had no choice but to follow their wishes. The boy simply had to accept that circumstances were out of his control.

Australia carries a long history of Aboriginal parents 'giving up' or 'taking' their children to missionaries or to state or federal governments. At least one-tenth of Aboriginal children were removed from their parents between 1910 and 1970, and these people are now referred to as the Stolen Generations. In the debate that followed the naming of these people as the Stolen Generations, and in a national report published in 1997 (Bringing Them Home: Report of the National Inquiry into the Separation of Aboriginal and Torres Strait Islander Children from Their Families), *some authorities suggested that there were documents to prove that the parents consented or did not object to their children being taken away. However, many parents had as little control of the situation as Dirimera had over the decision to go to Europe. In a situation they were powerless to change and a society that saw their culture as valueless, they did what they had to or what they thought was best for their children. Their options were narrow, and many who fought for their children lost them anyhow.*

The children who were taken were often told to forget where they came from so as to become 'Australian' and fit into white society. An advocate for Indigenous rights, Professor Mick Dodson, said, 'The best outcome, according to the authorities, depended on children being de-Aboriginalised if you like and made into white fellas. . . it was the official policy in some jurisdictions right up until the mid-1980s'.[1] Aboriginal children were taken from their families and put in state schools or missions almost as soon as Western Australia was settled. Conaci and Dirimera were among the first children taken away from their families to go overseas, and the first Aboriginal people to go to Europe.

Conaci's likely age when he left for Europe was just seven years. At about that age, my family moved from Victoria to New South Wales. This felt different from the moves we had made before. I had started school and had friends in the country town of Sale. I even liked some of my teachers. It was my first 'big move', the one where I had to leave friends behind and understood that the house was sold and that once that happened we could not go back inside. I laugh now when I remember being excited about crossing the state border——it seemed exotic and exciting. I soon liked our new home in Sydney and made friends fast, and very quickly the move seemed not to have changed life much. It was only years later that I realised how different life would have been if we had never left that country town.

Dirimera was about ten years old. When I was about Dirimera's age the time came for the family to move again—from Sydney to South Australia. I was secretly devastated, crying myself to sleep for weeks, but did not challenge my parents about it. By this age I knew that as it was beyond my control, there was no use complaining about it.

When I think of Dirimera and Conaci stepping onto a ship for the first time, I think of these two reactions—one boy looked only towards the excitement of newness, and the other saw a situation he was resigned to. Neither of them could have imagined the consequences of leaving their families behind. Just over a year ago they had seen a white person for the first time. Their limited schooling and time with Salvado had given them a mere taste of Western culture. Their real education about the wider world would begin as they set eyes on the blue expanse of the Indian Ocean.

Conaci and Dirimera saw the sea for the first time as they rode in a horse-drawn buggy from Perth to Fremantle. Salvado and the Secretary of the Colony, Dr Madden, talked loudly over the clap of horses' hooves and the groans of the wooden carriage, while the boys were left to murmur among themselves about what they saw. Where the boys came from there were only rivers and occasional waterholes, many of which were unapproachable because of the mythical serpents that lived beneath the water. The expanse of sea smelled very different from a waterhole. In the summer sun, the soft white foam on the waves shone as bright as a thousand stars.

The boys diverted their gaze from the sea only as the horses slowed down to walk their way through the streets of Fremantle. Lapped by the shimmering turquoise sea, Fremantle was a cluster of stone buildings on a slope leading to the town's hive of activity—the port. Beaches of white sand spread out on either side of the docks. People did not then gather on the sand, but crammed inside shops and guest houses or milled about in the streets. Bars and hotels prospered from the lively passing trade of sailors, traders and other opportunists. On seeing the monk, Madden and the Aboriginal children, some of the barflies waved, some of them made jokes and laughed and others did not even bat an eyelid—these men had seen far stranger things.

For unlike the more staid Perth, Fremantle was a noisy, smelly, seedy town with few pretences. People had money, spent it fast and then moved on—they wanted to live for the moment, and their responsibilities to that place or to others were few.

For Nyungar people, Fremantle was a place of sorrow. Those who lived there had been pushed off their traditional lands, and most of them survived by stealing and begging and slept on the streets or on the beach. Conaci and Dirimera saw for the first time Aboriginal men red-eyed and stumbling drunk, and supposed they had lost their minds. Their spoonful of wine at Mass had left them with no understanding of the effects of alcohol on the body and of what it could do to people who had lost direction in life.

When the buggy slowed, it was quickly surrounded by Aboriginal men and women begging for food. Conaci and Dirimera looked at Salvado for cues as to what to do. When Salvado had first set foot in Australia, the first word a Nyungar person said to him was '*maranga*'. In the Galician language this word means deception, and it startled the young monk. In the local Nyungar language '*maranga*' is a plea for food, or simply means hunger.[2] Salvado had at first tried to feed these people pieces of bread. Now he knew they were so numerous that this task was hopeless, and he attempted to ignore them.

While most people chose to look away, Conaci and Dirimera could not help but stare at Nyungar prisoners, chained together and sometimes wearing iron weights on their feet, who were marched down the streets of Fremantle on their way to court or the lock-up. The prison in Fremantle overflowed and these human chains were often being transported to a larger prison on Rottnest Island.

Madden and Salvado pointed out the smudge of land in the sea and told Conaci and Dirimera that according to Nyungar belief, Rottnest Island was originally attached to the mainland but broke free in a volcanic eruption. Now it was a disastrous place to be sent—often leading to early death or mental derangement. The boys listened as Salvado shouted over the din, entertaining Madden with stories of Aboriginal people he knew who had been sentenced to prison. Many Yuet men who ended up in prison were convicted for stealing sheep, and Salvado had appeared a few times in court to defend them. Salvado argued that if the shepherds had not appeared on the plains and driven kangaroos out of the area, there would be no killing of stock. In his view, the law was unjust because Yuets did not understand their supposed guilt. While his arguments about ownership of kangaroos largely fell on deaf ears, Salvado succeeded in persuading the court to release men into his supervision rather than send them to Rottnest.

Court proceedings indicate that Salvado continually emphasised the good conduct of Aboriginal people in general:

> I think it right to note that while these natives had been arrested for stealing sixteen sheep on one single occasion from some shepherds near our mission, they had often driven our flock to pasture without our losing a single head—indeed it sometimes happened that a lamb went astray and was brought back the next day by other natives who had chanced to find it. For a hungry native this requires a self-restraint amounting to heroism![3]

Not everyone was so fortunate, and the most common offence of these chained prisoners was stealing.

The coachman stopped the horses at the docks and people crowded around to see the group dismount. Picking up their cases, the boys followed Salvado down the jetty, looking at the sea under the boards beneath them. Once on deck they learned how to climb down a ladder into the bowels of the ship, throwing their bags down below and following Salvado's lead. Although they were booked as 'steerage' (the cheapest tickets, which would normally assign them to communal bunks), the Secretary of the Colony's influence allowed them to unload their belongings under the spare bunk in Salvado's cabin. The boys would share this single bed together, sleeping above their teacher and master.

On deck, the boys met Captain Robert Brown, who loudly and briefly welcomed them. Brown instructed his tanned and toughened crew that the Aboriginal students were to be looked after on the long voyage ahead.

A crowd gathered at the dock to see Salvado and the boys depart from Fremantle on the *Emperor of China* on 8 January 1849. Mostly Catholics gathered together by Bishop Brady, the assembled onlookers regarded Salvado as a local saint. Eight years earlier, on 12 December 1841, the passionate Catholic minority had begun their lobbying for priests and monks by writing a letter to Vicar-General William Ullathorne in Sydney:

We, the Catholics of Perth, West Australia, beg to call your attention to the following facts. In this and the surrounding towns, there are to be found all kinds of Protestant ministers who show a good deal of activity in preaching their creed … Not only do they try the conversion of the natives, but also endeavour to bring about the perversion of the Catholics by getting them to give up their religion. … Should a favourable opportunity present itself, they would, we believe come back to their faith. To us Catholics, our greatest, and, I dare say, our only joy would be to build a church and to have a priest sent us, whom we promise, we would support to the best of our means. Trusting that your Lordship will take this important matter into consideration, and that you will provide in all kindness for the salvation of our souls, Robert D'Arcy. On behalf of the Catholics of Perth.[4]

The assembled Catholics had long waited for charismatic leaders like Salvado and were concerned for his fate. They sang and kissed their rosary beads as he waved from aboard the ship. Nyungar beggars hung back and watched the scene, no doubt wondering how these two black boys had become so specially regarded and what would become of them at sea. Their youth, their full bellies, their European clothes all contrasted with the ragged, hungry look of the beggars, whose way of life had aged even the younger ones.

In a flurry, the ropes to the dock were gathered on deck, the anchor hauled on board and the sails drawn open. The *Emperor of China* swayed and lurched as the wind picked up the sails. As Salvado felt the vessel move out from the dock, he realised it was three years since he had set foot on Australian soil. For Conaci and Dirimera, it was just over a year since they had arrived at the mission and made Salvado's acquaintance.

⌒

The *Emperor of China* set its sails for the West. As it entered deeper waters, the ship began to sway from side to side and the boys had to sit down to keep from falling. The month in Perth had accustomed them to a less physically active life than at the mission, but for the next four months their world was a 90-foot-long vessel bordered by sea. Salvado told them to relax, settle back and keep out of the way of the sailors. Before the grand experiment could be furthered, they must have a great adventure at sea.

Conaci and Dirimera spent the first two or three days ill and nauseous. In the hull, vomit and sweat filled the humid air in a cloying manner that was often unbearable. When they climbed up to the deck, the boys were weak and moved slowly and shakily around the ship, breathing in the salty sea air. They were amazed at the expanse of water. Each day the sea seemed to change colour: one day it was green, the next blue, the day after that grey. While they were confined to the creaking wooden structure of the ship, all around them was infinite space and water.

The sea excited and terrified the boys. It was so massive, so wild and so untouchable—they could not drink the water, swim in the water, or escape the water. Even their own bodies surrendered to the water—grains of salt formed in the corners of their eyes, the wind blown off the waves dried and stiffened their hair, and when they sweated they no longer smelled themselves but the sea.

The crew largely worked around the boys without involving them in chores, as they were under instruction from the captain to treat them like any other guests aboard. The men who formed crews on ships like the *Emperor of China* were tough, and bonded through pranks and hardship. In the days when newcomers to the crew were tarred, feathered and shaved, and boys who showed signs of fear were chased up the ship's mast, it was lucky for Conaci and Dirimera that the protection of the captain shielded them from similar rough treatment. Salvado, too, could have been a target of derision from the largely Protestant crew.

Salvado tried to distract Conaci and Dirimera from their unease by making them pray and sing with him, which he did at set times of the day on deck. Salvado kneeled and chanted, oblivious to men running around him to set sails or pull aboard nets of fish. Salvado also continued the boys' instructions in languages so they would be ready for school in Europe.

Conaci and Dirimera preferred to spend all the time they could on deck, where the air was fresh and they could look for signs of life. Sometimes they followed schools of dolphins to the bow of the boat and watched them bounce out of the water, squeaking and dipping their noses mid-air as they raced to surf the ship's waves. At other times they climbed up on ropes and boxes to look down into the fishing nets that were hauled aboard, to see slimy octopuses, giant tuna, swordfish with long noses, writhing eels, and sometimes even the pointed teeth of small sharks.

The boys were often startled by the sight of flying fish. When chased by dolphins or large schools of tuna, these fish would jump and seem to fly through the air in arcs of 6 metres in length. They often landed on the deck of the ship, where they would sputter and gasp until they could no longer breathe, and the colour in their scales would slowly fade to grey.

One of Salvado's favoured pastimes was stringing lines from the back of the boat to catch albatross—which then existed in fourteen different Indian Ocean species—and the boys probably took part. This included the occasional catch of a Wandering Albatross, which has a wingspan of nearly 3.5 metres and a weight of up to 10 kilograms. More commonly, they caught albatrosses weighing about 2.5–3.5 kilograms, which the galley cook would roast like a chicken or goose. Salvado would reel in these birds to the deck. With the fishing hook and line caught down its throat, the albatross's hooked beak opened and closed as it squawked. Dirimera would sometimes step in to knock the bird out with a stone. The galley cook would come on deck to string up the bird and pluck it—a haze of black, white and grey feathers filled the air with a fleshy, oily smell.

At night, Conaci and Dirimera sometimes went up to the deck and just stared at the sea in darkness. In the Indian Ocean there is a natural phenomenon known as bioluminescence. The water in the wake of a ship shines fluorescently with light produced by millions of tiny living organisms, and it is believed that this wavy bright line in the sea may underlie the myth of giant sea serpents.

At the ship's helm, Conaci and Dirimera spent many hours in the company of Captain Brown and his son learning about sailing and navigation. They came to understand that the ship was indeed not an animal as they had originally thought. Instead they were taught about machines and other inventions that act as though they are alive but are controlled by men. They learned how the sails were used to steer the ship, and that the weight of the anchor could hold the vessel to the sea's floor.

After the boys ceased being ill and could walk around the ship, Brown showed them how he measured their longitude and distance to the Greenwich meridian using a sextant—an arc of 60 degrees used to sight altitude which, accompanied by a mathematical equation, can tell sailors their location on the globe. Conaci surprised everyone by being able to replicate the action after watching Brown do this just once. The captain laughed and made Conaci take the meridian four times that day to prove to an unbelieving crew that 'the darkie' could do it. The captain was amused that four of his men had taken months to take the meridian accurately while a 'native' picked it up in minutes.

Brown delighted the boys by letting them look through the telescope—an invention they understood as a new more powerful 'eye' than their own. It was through this lens that on 3 February the boys saw the first piece of land they had come across for twenty-six days. It was the island of Madagascar, 241 kilometres off in the distance— a brown smudge on the horizon.

Nine days later they were to long for land more than ever. At three in the afternoon the sky clouded dark, thunder cracked over their heads and lightning struck the sea's surface. The boys looked on in shock as two sailors at the bow of the ship were bowled over by a wave that slid them across the deck as though they were flotsam and jetsam. The rain began to pour as waves rushed past, and Captain Brown reversed the sails so that the ship remained firm in the midst of the squall. Salvado took the boys below deck, where the passengers were frightened and many of them violently ill.

At sunrise, Salvado, Conaci and Dirimera cautiously peered out, to find that the rain had stopped. The waves still rose, as Salvado put it, 'like high walls that we could not possibly surmount and then gave way to abysses from which it looked as if we would never emerge'.[5] Later that day the waves slowly began to soften and the ship would make its way at 8 knots as the waves rushed past in the opposite direction at 32 knots. The boys were called to the deck to see another extraordinary sight—the first ship they had seen since setting out from Fremantle thirty-six days earlier. It was making its way slowly from Calcutta to London.

Two days later another blur of land defined by a peak was seen one hundred kilometres in the distance. This was Table Mountain, and it signified that their first stop, South Africa, was near.

If the real was not fantastic enough, on 18 February the boys were to see their first mirage at sea. When there is a strong change of temperature beyond the horizon, the refraction of light can cause a rare mirage, known as a superior mirage. This mirage creates the illusion of distant objects being upside down in the sky. To Conaci and Dirimera's eyes, two ships following the *Emperor of China* were seen reflected in the air above, with taller sails than the real ships. To both the naked eye and the telescope there appeared to be four ships following them, two of which floated belly-up in the sky—like dead fish.

The following day, Conaci and Dirimera had been promised the sight of land without the help of a telescope, but a fog had settled over the water. The boys squinted and peered, trying to see the green land in the distance, as the ship cut through the grey mist. As they approached the shore, they saw an abandoned shipwreck on the rocks that jutted along the shallower waters. Turned on its side, which had torn and filled with water, the ship's mast pointed out almost horizontally at the mountains ahead, which circled a wide bay. This wreck-littered harbour, on what was known as the Cape of Good Hope, signalled their arrival in Cape Town. After forty-seven days at sea, on 19 February 1849, Conaci and Dirimera were eagerly anticipating walking on dry land.

Africa

It was the first time Conaci and Dirimera had seen mountains. As the ship approached Cape Town, one of the most famous port cities in the world, they looked up at the peaks surrounding the bay. Lion's Head was before them on their right, an upturned cone of rock, and steep mountains rose on their left. They stared at these dramatic shapes of land that made the white, ordered Georgian buildings of the settlement stretching along the arc of the bay look puny and fragile.

Over four hundred merchant ships sailed in and out of the bay every year, on their way from Europe to Asia and back again. Vessels were anchored all around the harbour, and row boats ferried merchants and sailors to and fro. Most of the crews were from Britain, and shouted to each other in English over the sound of fluttering sails, swaying masts, ships' horns and the creaking of vessels in the wind and the waves.

The *Emperor of China* docked near the jetty, which formed a trail to a small castle. The spire of St George's church, a classical building modelled on St Pancras church in London, could be seen in the distance—as could the formidable white, boxy barracks and the smoke billowing from the iron coaling station.[1]

Conaci and Dirimera followed Salvado and Madden down the ship's ramp to the jetty. Around them, men loaded and unloaded crates of Welsh coal, Burmese teak, China tea and Indian spices—but most of all, wool. It was bound for the textile mills of Europe. The Cape of Good Hope alone shipped out 5000 pounds (about 2300 kilograms) of wool worth £199 432 in 1849, and over the next ten years this amount would quadruple.[2] Australia, like South Africa, had imported merino sheep, and competition for wool markets had for some time been hard fought. The wealth of both colonies was won 'off the sheep's back'.

The noises and smells of cargo, live animals and people being transported, plus the shouts of sailors and traders, created a din above which Salvado barely had time to instruct the boys to stay close. As soon as they put foot on the Cape's shore, Conaci and Dirimera were surrounded by people of all skin colours asking them questions in various languages.

For this was one of the most racially diverse settlements anywhere in the British Empire. The Dutch, who had settled the Cape in the 1600s, and the more recently settled English were intermingling to form a new settler society in which the Dutch elite rose through the ranks of the English military, bureaucracy and industry. Journalist John Fairbairn wrote of the Dutch and English at the time, 'Their interests are identical, and cannot be separated, or opposed to each other without equal injury to both. By local intermixture, by intermarriages and by connections in business, these two classes have, to a great extent, lost their original distinctions.'[3]

Dominated by the white settlers were the indigenous black South Africans—many of them displaced and interned as servants or slaves. To the English and Dutch, the local Khoikhoi people were referred to as 'Hottentots', which soon became a derogatory name. The Khoikhoi men wore soft hats, long-sleeved shirts and trousers. The women piled their hair up on their heads, spiralling it around and around and then wrapping it in brightly coloured cloth. They wore loose-fitting smocks and dresses that entirely covered their bodies, and swayed as they walked. They were darker than Conaci and Dirimera and stared at the boys' curious clothes.

The black slaves were often from Madagascar and Mozambique, brought over by the Dutch. They lived in groups and held their own dances on Sundays, where they mingled with the local Khoikhoi. On the docks, some

Khoikhoi and African slaves asked Conaci and Dirimera, 'Where are you from?' They tried to finger the boys' fine hair, a key signifier to them that these boys were different.

Malays also joined the crowd of the curious around the Aboriginal boys. The Dutch had, since the seventeenth century, imported the majority of slaves in the Cape from all over their empire in the Indian Ocean, but especially from the Dutch East Indies (now Malaysia and Indonesia). This meant that most of the Malay slave population and their descendants were Muslims, and soon there were six thousand of them on the Cape of Good Hope. The Muslim holy leaders wore turbans around their heads, and many other Malays wore a pointy 'Chinaman's hat'. The Malays were entrepreneurial, operating their businesses outside the elite's circle of influence and building their own mosques. They were puzzled by the reddish tinge of the boys' hair and asked Conaci and Dirimera, 'Are you half-caste?'

About half the Cape's population were people of mixed race, and the children of the Dutch, English, Germans, Malays and Africans were all colours, shapes and sizes. Yet Conaci and Dirimera were curiosities to them.

Madden and Salvado wrestled the boys away from the crowds. They made their way into the bustling town. They passed the docks and the narrow-windowed Malay houses, which smelt of molasses and whale oil—a mix of which Malay people used to waterproof their roofs. They walked through Greenmarket Square, where Malays and Africans had created makeshift tents by stringing sheets of cotton over a few long sticks to cover their fruit, vegetables and other basic fare. They passed the African Theatre in Hottentot Square, a long hall approached by stairs at its front entrance that served as a concert hall, a school for freed slaves on Sundays and a church.

Throughout the city itself, order and Dutch neatness prevailed. Cape Town prospered, thanks to the export of African resources and the influx of sailors and ships bound for Europe and Asia. The city was attractive to European eyes, as Salvado recorded: 'Spacious squares, beautiful gardens and delightful avenues bordered by a double line of pine and other trees, place this city, as regards its beauty, on a par with the best provincial cities of Europe'.[4]

Paintings and drawings of the time depict two versions of the city. The artist Thomas Bowler created images of the Cape Town that Salvado saw—he showed pictures of order, industry and self-improvement for Dutch and English settlers, Africans and Asians alike. Charles Davidson Bell depicted the Khoikhoi drunk, the black men and women fighting and their children distressed. He mirrored many settlers' perceptions in his popular painting *Jan van Riebeeck Meets the Hottentots*, in which Riebeeck, together with a trader, a preacher and two soldiers, boldly faces a group of dishevelled Khoikhoi.[5]

Which of these images Conaci and Dirimera would have found closer to the truth is impossible to know. If they had seen the Cape Town street scenes that inspired

Bell's depictions of drunken Khoikhoi, the boys might well have recalled the lost, landless Nyungars living on the fringes of Fremantle.

Walking down the central streets, they and Salvado came across a regimental band. The sound of this music thrilled the boys. They had never heard anything like it before and wanted to follow the music, imitating the marching of the band members and falling into line behind them. Salvado had to insist they leave, but that short exposure to European music left a great impression on Conaci and Dirimera: 'For many days afterwards they kept on imitating the motions of the players, and trying to reproduce the sounds of the music with their voices'.[6]

On their first night in the Cape, the boys sat at the table with Salvado and Bishop Griffith, Vicar Apostolic of Mauritius, and the men talked Church politics. Salvado was alarmed to learn that Serra had been consecrated Bishop of Port Victoria (Darwin), which meant that the mission would be managed by new and probably inexperienced hands. He had not originally wanted to come to Europe, for fear that in his absence the mission would be neglected and all his work would be for nothing.

Like New Norcia, the missions in Mauritius that Bishop Patrick Griffith spoke of had become well established and had encountered few opponents. Salvado recounted the story of his first contact with people from the Yuet tribe. As Salvado described it, the first night he spent alone in the Australian bush with a group of Yuets sleeping nearby was perilous: 'At the thought, however, that our guests were cannibals, we found that sleep deserted us for the night'.[7] However, two days later, after they had been observed by the Yuets and vice versa without communicating, the missionaries gathered a lot of damper, tea and sugar, knelt and asked for God's blessing, then approached the crowd. The glistening men tensed and seized their weapons, the women and children ran away in fear. The missionaries held their ground and ate the food they held to demonstrate what they were offering. It did not take long before they were understood by the Yuet men:

> Some of them lowered their weapons and Father Serra and I handed out sugar and bread, paying special attention to some small boys who were crying and clinging to their parents' legs and showing every sign of terror. When they first tried the sugar they spat it out suspiciously but, seeing that we were quite happy about it, they tried some more, found they liked it, nodded their heads in signs of approval and encouraged the others to eat. In a few minutes, they had disposed of all we had to spare and were quarrelling over the precious remnants.
>
> Work was suspended for the rest of that day, so excited were we at the happy turn of events. Some of the natives went back with us to the hut, where we showed them our agricultural implements and made them gape in surprise. That night we said special prayers of thanks and went to sleep in peace.[8]

As Salvado told stories, Conaci and Dirimera ate in silence. Their hot dinner must have seemed luxurious after the previous month's diet of dried meat, non-perishable foods and what could be caught at sea. They ate using the forks and knives, a skill that Salvado had taught them as one way of whiling away the long hours on the ship. Every now and then they would glance curiously at the servants coming from the kitchen—the women with clothes wrapped around their heads and the men with skin blacker than theirs.

The next days were spent visiting the town's clergy and elite as Salvado talked excitedly about the boys and their endeavour to become monks. He told tales of the success of the mission—a subject of interest, since most missionaries who ventured north from the Cape were killed, starved or returned defeated.

The other topic of conversation on Madden's mind was the slowly emerging anti-convict movement. A few months after their stay, this issue would erupt in the Cape and cause a political deadlock. The previous year Earl Grey, Secretary of State for the Colonies,[9] had resumed transportation of convicts to New South Wales and established the Cape as a penal settlement, and in 1849 two hundred convicts were sent there. However, the Anti-Convict Association argued that convicts would increase crime and social conflict in their city. They held large demonstrations, involving as many as seven thousand people at a time, in the central streets and squares of

Cape Town.[10] In Perth, Madden had dealt with similar anti-convict protests and had had to pacify opposition with the proviso that convicts would do public works rather than being released at large.[11]

To quench Salvado's thirst for knowledge of other missions, he and the boys visited local churches. Although the Portuguese Catholics had reached the Cape before the Dutch, building a small chapel at Mossel Bay in 1501, the Catholic presence was gone by the 1600s and the Dutch East India Company forbade the practice of Catholicism. The Dutch Reformed Church, or Nederduitse Gereformeerde Kerk (NGK), soon dominated the Cape, until British churches arrived in the 1700s.

By the time Salvado, Conaci and Dirimera arrived in the Cape there was conflict about whether the NGK should preach only to white settlers or seek to convert the Khoikhoi people. Many white churchgoers were against the idea of missions, because the doctrine that everyone is equal in the eyes of God would threaten the racial divide on which they depended for labour and land. The NGK was torn between those who supported the Synod of 1829 that ordered that Holy Communion be given 'to all members without distinction of colour or origin', and the ideas of German theologian Abraham Kuyper that there were orders in creation that justified separate spheres of sovereignty and treatment for different classes of people.

The pro-Kuyper views that Madden and Salvado discussed in the Cape were soon to become embedded in

NGK policy and the political consciousness of white settlers known as Afrikaners.[12] They were the intellectual underpinnings of a system that would become formalised as Apartheid in the twentieth century and would traumatise the nation of South Africa.

Salvado describes a strange encounter that occurred during their visit to South Africa between Conaci and Dirimera and a 'deranged Malay woman'. When she joined a crowd around the boys asking questions about where they were from, Salvado explained that Conaci and Dirimera were on their way to England. On hearing this news, the Malay woman clutched the boys' arms and, running, led them away. But Conaci and Dirimera were frightened of her. They scratched and hit her, fighting their way free, and ran back to Salvado, grabbing onto his robes for protection. The red-eyed Malay woman called after them, 'If you go to Britain, you will be murdered!'[13]

Salvado and the boys farewelled their church friends and the continent of Africa on 24 February, and boarded the newly stocked *Emperor of China*. The ship set its sails northwestward. After being followed by crowds of inquisitive people for the past five days, the ship must have seemed tranquil to the boys.

When Conaci and Dirimera next saw land, it was a lonely barren island that the British had named St Helena.

From a distance, the only mountain—Diane, rising over 900 metres from the sea—seemed bare. As they approached the island, Conaci and Dirimera realised that this was not just a trick caused by distance—the island's landscape was barren and its basalt had coloured it a dark grey. The ship docked at Jamestown, a set of whitewashed and stone buildings lining a single main street that ran in a straight line at the bottom of two steep slopes of basalt. In contrast to the green, alluring mountains surrounding Cape Town, the fiercely plain complexion of St Helena almost urged sailors to continue past it.

The town survived because this 16-kilometre-long island was the only land to be had in the Atlantic Ocean between South Africa and South America. The island, nearly 2000 kilometres from Africa and nearly 3000 from Brazil, was kept alive by the trade of passing ships from Europe, Latin America, Asia and Australia. Discovered by Portuguese admiral Joao da Nova in 1502, from 1659 it came under British control, except for a brief Dutch occupation. The British East India Company had a substantial landholding on the island.

As Conaci and Dirimera made their way into the small settlement, they were met with brief glances but no questions or particular hostility. With just five thousand people living there, St Helena had the character of a small English village. In 1775 Captain James Cook summed up this feeling, remarking that Saint Helenians were 'the most hospitable ever met with of English extraction, having scarce any tincture of avarice and ambition'.[14] For black St Helenians, this trait was to be exploited. Many were taken to the Cape of Good Hope in the 1840s because they were regarded as more 'docile' than the local indigenous people and more suitable as servants. Other Africans came to St Helena as slaves bound for the Americas, on ships that were intercepted by the British. Freed on this remote island, ex-slaves had few options other than to seek work locally until they gathered enough money for a ticket elsewhere.

St Helena's society was soon dominated by all things English, and to Salvado's disappointment there was not a single Catholic priest or church on the island. Jamestown had just two Protestant churches.

After walking through the town with the other passengers, Salvado and the boys made their way to a house where Napoleon Bonaparte had lived upon first being exiled to St Helena. The small building stood near a waterfall not far from the shore but a safe distance from Jamestown, which could be seen in the valley below. The passengers of the *Emperor of China* then moved on to the main tourist attraction, the house where Napoleon had spent the last six years of his life. The dry slopes added to the heat and dust of the climb to the top of the high plateau where the house stood. Salvado and the boys stopped to rest and to view the fortress and the sea in the distance before going inside.

Salvado later described the house where Napoleon contemplated his life in his last years as 'completely dilapidated and derelict'. The place where he was first buried was being used as a horse stable, and the site of the tomb was covered in rotting straw, with only an iron railing around it to mark the spot. Around the site stood a solitary cypress tree and three weeping willows. Salvado attempted to explain the significance of Napoleon, 'a great leader and ruler of Western Europe', to Conaci and Dirimera. He considered the scene about them to be a poor reflection of Napoleon's life: 'This man who was once the arbiter of Europe's destiny, who was victorious in a hundred battles, who made and unmade so many kings, ended his days an exile in this far-away spot!'[15]

Conaci and Dirimera would have been less surprised than Salvado by the unassuming grave of Napoleon at St Helena. In their culture, the dead were carefully prepared for their next journey—the corpse was bound with grass and wrapped in kangaroo skin, weapons and food were placed alongside, and a large stone was put on top to crush the bones. A fire was lit near the corpse to keep the dead person's spirit warm for the first few days after their death. But there was no gravestone or marker of the place of burial. The earth itself was more significant than the person whom it covered, and when sites were sacred it was because of their significance to spirits or to the tribe, not to an individual.

Napoleon's remains were retrieved from the barren land of St Helena nineteen years after his death. His body was returned to France, where it now has pride of place in the Hotel des Invalides in Paris. It is one of the most ornate, elaborate and assuming tombs in Western Europe. Descending the stairs to the circular tomb, the temperature drops as visitors approach a heavy bronze door forged from cannons retrieved from his successful battle at Austerlitz against the Russians and Austrians. As the door opens, visitors step onto a mosaic that depicts the main battles of Napoleon's empire, and twelve men of victory lean against the pillars to hold up the roof of the tomb.

In this heavy, enclosed space, the sarcophagus sits on a green granite pedestal. There Napoleon lies. Those who saw his body being transported from St Helena made the dubious claim that when he was unearthed he was 'perfectly preserved'. He was reportedly dressed in his colonel's uniform and draped with the sash of the Légion d'honneur to be entombed in Paris inside six coffins— one of soft iron, another of mahogany, two made of lead, one of ebony and the last and outer one of oak.

This was all built to record the life and achievement of a maker of modern history. He conquered much of Europe and North Africa, introduced the concept of the conscript army, spread revolutionary and nationalist ideals, and created laws that still exist in the form of the Napoleonic Code.

When I last visited, his tomb seemed to have an added significance—it is a temple to the primacy that Western culture places on the individual. It celebrates individual achievements and individual power in its opulence and style. If you think of all the soldiers who died in his battles, they are still seen as his battles; if you think of all the work that went into making this sarcophagus, this temple, it is still Napoleon's coffin, Napoleon's temple. If you think about yourself at all, it is along the lines of a quip by one American tourist, 'It's a hell of a lot different than what we did for Grandma'. Inevitably, weighed against such a monument, other individual lives feel ordinary and insignificant.

In old age, Aboriginal people acquire enormous respect. They become known as 'elders' and are to be listened to and heard. They frequently become the glue holding families together in hard times and helping to care for children. They are recognised not necessarily for individual achievement but for having passed so many years on the planet and seen so many events and people come and go. Experience itself is valued and honoured. Conaci and Dirimera knew that if they grew up and became old, they too would be elders and would be respected for their knowledge. In death as in life they would simply, but not unimportantly, become part of the communal landscape. To Conaci and Dirimera, the idea that anything extra could be expected to mark their passing was novel.

The following day, 9 March 1849, Conaci and Dirimera were back on board the *Emperor of China*. Six days later they saw another island through the telescope—the volcanic peak of Ascension Island. And alongside Ascension Island they sighted the largest animals they had ever seen. Whales, in small schools, broke the surface of the ocean and squirted water into the air. In the turquoise water, their huge bodies were dark blue shadows that broke the water with their immense weight. When the whales were especially close, Conaci and Dirimera could feel the vibration in the water made by their calls to one another. One whale swam right beside the ship, revealing its round eye as it expelled air and water through its blowhole. The boys, along with Salvado, spent time 'observing it at close quarters for more than ten minutes' before it swam away, flicking its tail against the water's surface.

The ship crossed the Equator on 20 March. The successful crossing was a cause for celebration by the crew. For new crew members, it was a rite of passage—the others would gather the rookies together and 'christen' them. This christening could be plastering their bodies with tar, dipping them in feathers and then shaving their bodies, so that their skin was raw and beset with 'sailors scars'. Or it would be pressuring boys to drink until they passed out on deck. Some galley boys would only sail between Africa and Australia to avoid such rites of passage, and also due to the commonly held belief that it was dangerous to cross the Equator because it was so hot there that the sea would boil. Conaci and Dirimera crossed the line at eight in the evening, and the cheers of the crew were largely dimmed by the sound of pouring rain on deck.

As Easter approached, Salvado abstained from meats and fish and increased the boys' prayers and religious instruction. In the early evening of 5 April a host of cuttlefish descended on the boat. They seemed to be propelled through the air by the strength of their long, waving tentacles. The crew gathered them up and the cook served them the next day for breakfast, but the boys and Salvado could not taste them because it was Good Thursday. As they celebrated Easter with Mass for the few Catholics aboard the ship, the nearest land was East Africa or Cuba.

For two days of the following week, the ship cut through vast schools of bluebottles, commonly known at the time as 'Portuguese men of war'. Conaci and Dirimera looked down to see the surface of the sea clouded over with their blue and pink bodies; their pink-ridged crests waved on the surface while their fat blue bodies dangled coiled stinging tentacles that could be longer than 10 metres. An inexperienced galley boy dipped his hands into the sea to pick one up, and was in 'intense pain' until rum was applied to his burns and blisters, the alcohol taking some of the sting out of the wound.

Gradually the boys left the turquoise tropical seas behind them, and by 12 April the *Emperor of China* had reached the same latitude as Lisbon. The next day they could no longer see the islands of the Azores and were sailing at the latitude of southern France, not far from the isles of Great Britain.

Great Britain

nce turquoise and bright, the sea had lost its colour, becoming darker and greyer as the ship approached the British Isles. The spring air was crisp and the boys took out extra shirts from their trunks in order to keep warm. Some days the sky would seem close and heavy, on other days blue would peak through the clouds as they drifted past. Storms often made it too dangerous for Conaci and Dirimera to go on deck and they waited in the galley, listening to the crew sing old songs, joke and make plans about what they would do when they went ashore. Days were long and dull on that last part of their journey. There was no land to be sighted and the weather was too rough for play on deck. Salvado tried to keep the boys lively with lessons, sometimes conducted as the three of them lay on their beds, the ship swaying all around them and Salvado shouting over the sound of water—water underneath them, beside them and crashing in waves over them on the deck.

It was in European waters that Dirimera learned the seductive danger of the waves. As he stood on deck and watched one rise high, almost as high as the top quarter of the mast, he lost his balance in the lurch of the vessel. He fell, hitting his head. As the waves crashed around him, Dirimera lay flat on the deck and still as the dead. Salvado described him as being 'unconscious for several minutes'. When he came to, revived by Conaci and Salvado, Dirimera's vision was blurred and his eyes stung with salt. He was dazed and erratic for a few days afterwards.

Two weeks later, after Dirimera had recovered from his headaches and regained his sea legs, it seemed almost surreal, after 109 days on the *Emperor of China*, to finally leave the sea and sail up the Welsh River Tarve on 27 April. On the shore to their left was Swansea—then a grid of terraced and uniform buildings that made up the shops, homes, bars and other amenities of the city. To their right, warehouses and factories sat in neat squares puffing out fat and putrid plumes of smoke that hung low in the clouded sky. The sailors cheered at this unimpressive sight.

Conaci and Dirimera farewelled Captain Brown, who had been a patient teacher to them while they were at sea. He patted Conaci on the back with particular fondness and some concern for the clever young thing who knew so little of where he was. The boys left the *Emperor of China* behind as they descended a rickety ladder after Salvado, his monk's robes rushing around his body in the wind. Conaci and Dirimera jumped into a waiting rowboat.

The Welshman at the helm murmured in a thick accent and rowed Salvado, the boys and Madden's family right up to the edge of the city. Conaci and Dirimera set their shaky feet onto the grey pebbled shore. Their bodies swayed with confusion at their new surrounds and they had to sit to stop the dizziness. While the boys rested on a ledge, Salvado farewelled Dr Madden, who was on his way to London. Madden's young son, Thomas, bid them a formal farewell as the people around them looked suspiciously at the black boys in grey Swansea.

As they moved into the city, the air hung heavy around their dazed heads. A dense grey haze of smoke, dust and metal filled the air. When the rain fell in soft drops on their skin, it coated Conaci and Dirimera in grey, sticky soot and ash. The distant hills were orange and beige and, when the boys looked closer at them, they realised the landscape was treeless.

Swansea had stripped the life from its surrounds. Producing coal, copper and tin, it was a key centre of the British mining industry. The city of 40 000 serviced southern Wales by refining and exporting goods from the green, insular countryside. The fields wilted and dried brown on the barren hills around the city. The cows there often had to be slaughtered because their joints thickened and their teeth rotted. Pollution was recognised but, in Britain's quest to hold on to economic might, was ignored by the authorities.

Conaci and Dirimera walked past one of the tinplate factories—the region pumped out nearly 40 000 tonnes of tinplate a year. They saw barrow girls, some as young as themselves, wheeling barrows of metal to the fat brick columns that were the furnaces. Legislation had recently saved children from working underground in the mines, but this work was equally arduous.

The men who greeted the barrow girls at the furnace had leathery faces running with sweat. They had to drink gallons of water each day to survive the extreme heat. Once the metal had been passed through the furnace, boys handled the finished product—packing and preparing it for transport. It must have made the chores that Conaci and Dirimera had become accustomed to on the mission seem light work in comparison.

Over the next few days, Conaci and Dirimera could not have helped but notice that the workers of Swansea coughed loudly and were often out of breath. Each house echoed with the fighting and laughter of at least five or six people sharing a roof. Since each house was joined to another on both sides, in rows of two-bedroom terraces, the muggy streets hummed with muffled sounds of life.

The people of the city worked hard and kept to themselves—unlike the curiosity of the Cape or the laid-back friendliness of St Helena, Swansea was uninterested

in newcomers. Visiting English people often made fun of
the Welsh and their situation, as in this verse about the
industrial area of Landore:

> It came to pass in days of yore
> The Devil chanced upon Landore
> Quoth he, 'By all this fume and stink
> I can't be far from home I think'.[1]

Salvado and the boys, once again a trio on their own,
based themselves at the Benedictine church in St David's
Place in the centre of town. A Catholic mission had been
established in Protestant Swansea forty years previously,
when Abbé Séjean, once a chaplain to Louis XVI, fled
France after the revolution. But when Conaci and Dirimera
arrived, the church was just a year old—built by the
Benedictines with savings, borrowings and the proceeds of
fundraising exercises such as tea parties. Gothic in style,
with a long, steep slate roof and stone walls, the church
looked like any other in the countryside at the time. It
was there that they celebrated a late Easter Mass, Salvado
excited to once again be among his Benedictine brethren.

The other monks were eager to welcome him and to
hear more about the faraway mission of New Norcia, and
Salvado desperately needed their support after the long
journey at sea. Father Kavanagh took the three visitors in
at a house nearby and managed to get them some pounds
to spend, as Salvado was almost broke.

Conaci and Dirimera alarmed Salvado when they pointed out a person on the street whose face was covered with pustules. Smallpox was rife in Great Britain. The most infectious of all known infectious fevers, it could be spread through breathing near contaminated clothing or other common items, and by necessity the poor shared everything. First, people fell ill and their faces ran red with fever and sweat. Then their faces erupted into red bumps, and by the eighth day these red bumps swelled into putrid yellow pustules and everyone knew it was smallpox. Those who survived would always bear deep pitted scars all over their faces—some scars red, others bruised and purple.

Salvado began a campaign to protect the boys from the disease—eventually finding a willing man he described as Dr Long of Swansea, who inoculated the boys for free. The jab was short and deep. It drew blood, and both the boys had bandages around their left shoulders like soldiers. When the bandages were wound out and removed a few days later, the boys compared arms—both would forever have a small, round scar on their left shoulder, and they laughed about being 'blood brothers'.

Boys of their age at home may have had rows of lines tattooed on their arms and chest. Although it was not obligatory, many Nyungars, and particularly the men, tattooed themselves using pieces of quartz to cut vertical lines on their arms and legs. On their chests and shoulders they scraped horizontal lines of up to 150 millimetres in length. The scars created ridges across their skin, and the higher these rose from the cuts the more attractive they were seen to be. Now, instead of the tribe's markings, Conaci and Dirimera had acquired the scars of modern medicine.

After a few days charming the local Catholics and the elite of Swansea, Salvado's charismatic persona helped them yet again when he secured a free ticket for himself and the boys to Liverpool and Dublin, from 'Miss Mary Nicholl and her sister'. So, after a short time in Wales, they again set out to sea.[2]

⌒

Underneath my feet as I walked on the shore of Swansea were grey, round stones flecked with pieces of red brick and shavings of shiny metal. The odd piece of green glass made round by the sea interrupted this monotony. The debris of the beach is trampled by only a few—an old man and his dog, a woman with her face pursed against the wind.

Once a key port and industrial city, Swansea is now left alone. Its museum is largely empty, its signs and displays reminding the curious few that the city, less than two hundred years ago, held thousands of people who depended on its industry. The churches are insular affairs with few grandiose features, but with heavy stone walls and roofs held up by beams that seem to hunch in apathy at their circumstances.

As in Conaci and Dirimera's time, the hills around Swansea are still unassuming, although after the decline of the factories and the emptying of minerals from the countryside, greenery is returning. The trees are still young and the fields are left to flounder with little purpose.

The lively part of town is its shopping mall, where women become animated and frantic, children scamper and teenagers flirt—by being as fierce as possible to one another, their chins jutted out, their shoulders slouched against walls.

Outside Swansea I visit the domain of men—one of the few remaining profitable coal mines in Wales. Once its key industry early last century, coal mining soon went the way of most of the mining industry—layoffs, outpricing by other countries, market downturns and a general slide into a globalised world where local was no longer viable.

I went down in the 'cage', literally a wire floor-to-roof elevator that descends into the mine. The air became tighter as we descended and the smell was damp. When the cage opened, I saw that the mine tunnels had not changed for centuries. Black coal was all around and it looked so silken in the orange light from our helmets that I wanted to touch it, but when I did my fingers were streaked in black. The miners do not care. Their hands instead of being pale on the palms are black; only the backs of their hands are white, because they so rarely see the sun.

There is something alien about being in a natural place that is entirely black. Without the torches, it would surely be the darkest place on earth. Generations of men spent their days in such places, and I wondered if this experience shaped the Welsh sensibility or whether it was naturally suited to it. I asked the two men, one young and just starting out and the other older and well familiar with the mine, 'Are you ever scared down here?'

They both assured me that they were not, that it felt perfectly fine, and I believed this reply. The Welsh, like their landscape, have an especially marked dual reality—one on the surface and one below the surface. Even though they are often aloof and reserved towards newcomers, once they begin talking to an outsider, information rushes out of them like a river—one that you get the impression usually only flows underground, within themselves.

Conaci and Dirimera's understanding of the world must have been turned upside down in Swansea, by the strange nature of the people, their dense accent, the grey skies and the city's industrialisation. In turn, they were viewed very differently than before. In Victorian Britain, the whole concept of children and childhood was very different to that in Australia at the time or in Britain today. Play and learning were less important than quickly filling your slot in life. Children were functional creatures, not beings in their own right. In this perspective, Conaci and Dirimera were oddities—their function had not been set by their parents, their class or their colour, but by one man's view.

In Britain, if children were from rich families, they were groomed and educated to take over the business, property and inheritance of their parents. If they were from poor families, children went out to factories and earned a wage—as Conaci and Dirimera had first learned in Swansea and were about to again discover in the dark and dense streets of Liverpool.

Liverpool made Swansea look provincial in comparison. It was the largest settlement Conaci and Dirimera had seen. As they sighted it from the ship, they could not have helped but be impressed by the stately trade buildings in the distance, which were white, Georgian and massive. The pale grey dome of the Customs House rose above the many-storeyed red-brick buildings that held banks, shops and markets and spread across the horizon.

Their ship travelled towards the city on the Mersey River, dark as liver and called 'the Pool'. Another theory about how Liverpool got its name attributes it to the large number of eels in the Mersey, the original name of which was thought to have been 'elverpool'. Conaci and Dirimera looked down the side of the ship at the reflection of their surprised faces shining back at them from the black water, like a mirror.

They entered the docks with the rush of traffic at high tide. This was the world's first wet dock, built a century before. The gates to the dock were opened at high tide, then closed to stop the tide draining the Pool. Ships could unload and load in one and a half days rather than the two weeks needed when the low tide was allowed to transform the harbour into a shallow pool. Without this invention, shipping would have been far less efficient and Liverpool would never have been able to develop as a key centre in Britain's Industrial Revolution.

As their ship moved closer to the shore and the gates closed through the water behind them, the still water in the brick-walled docks and canals was cut rough by the volume of vessels passing through. Accounting for a reported third of Britain's export trade and a quarter of its import trade, an estimated one of every ten ships around the world hailed from Liverpool. Most ships had been at sea for months—sailing from Australia, North America, India and South Africa. The crews shouted at each other and ran around the decks in their impatience to unload their goods and themselves into the city.

As Conaci and Dirimera got off the ship, men from a neighbouring vessel dropped crates. When they hit the bricks, these boxes created clouds of white dust. Conaci asked what that wool-like fibre was, whose dust filled the air.

It was cotton and it was everywhere in Liverpool. Since the end of the slave trade in 1807, the city's fortunes had been made from importing white, tufty cotton fibres and spinning and manufacturing them into cloth. In the thirty years before Conaci and Dirimera arrived in Liverpool, the amount of cotton brought into the city had tripled, to 1.5 million bales a year. Workers followed, and increased the city's size from 250 000 to 400 000 people in the last ten years alone. Filling the mills, workers—mostly women and children—toiled at giant looms for long hours. Only two years earlier a national law had been introduced to limit hours of work to ten a day for women and children, but many still worked longer.

The meagre pay people received was taken at an increasing cost to their health as each day passed in those great sheds of spinners, weavers and factory hands. Inside the mills, the cotton fibres blanketed workers and filled the air around them. Every breath they took felt as though it was inhaled from under a suffocatingly dirty sheet that covered their faces. Their eyes swelled and blurred. Their chests felt tight and tired and they often developed lung disease.

If people did not die due to their conditions at work, it was usually due to the state of their homes and streets. The rapid expansion of the city had seen little planning, and the state of the sanitation could not have escaped the boys' noses. A doctor had reported on Liverpool at the time:

> In the streets inhabited by the working classes, I believe that the great majority are without sewers, and that where they do exist they are of a very imperfect kind unless where the ground has a natural inclination, therefore the surface water and fluid refuse of every kind stagnate in the street and add, especially in the hot weather, their pestilential influence to that of the more solid filth. With regard to the courts [dead-end streets], I doubt whether there is a single court in Liverpool which communicates with the street by an underground drain, the only means afforded

for carrying off the fluid dirt being a narrow, open, shallow gutter, which sometimes exists, but even this is very generally choked up with stagnant filth.[3]

Diseases such as cholera festered in these conditions. Some of the sick were admitted to 'fever hospitals' overrun with patients. Many more died in their homes at an early age. One official reported that 60 per cent of deaths recorded in the city were of infants under five years of age.[4]

Despite the familiarity with misery, or perhaps because of it, Liverpool was a loud, raucous place. The people who lived there were confronting, honest and argumentative. Conaci and Dirimera strained their ears to listen to the Scouse accent, thick and short, mixed with the lilting debates of the Irish that emanated from the many public bars of the city as they passed. The boys looked curiously into the black-beamed rooms decked out with soggy leather and wood chairs, where pale-skinned and lean bodies perched their exaggerated potbellies.

Pubs had sprung up like flourishing bulbs as the city grew. This was a scandal according to Ramsay Muir, who wrote at the time:

On the sacred principles of free trade, it was held, there should be no distinction drawn between beer shops and bread shops and open competition would rectify all evils. There might have been something to say for this view if

the appetite for beer had been, like the appetite for bread—
a natural appetite with natural limits.[5]

The workers who filled the pubs, textile mills and docks
came from all over. Some were ex-slaves. A small population
of a few thousand Africans was well established by the
time Conaci and Dirimera visited, so that many Liverpudlians would have assumed that they too were from
Africa. However, most of the new citizens of Liverpool
came from Ireland. Three years earlier, at the height of
the Irish potato famine in 1846, many people were forced
to leave their country to find work and so survive. That
year, 90 000 Irish people entered Liverpool in the first
three months. An estimated extra 300 000 arrived in
Liverpool in 1847 and they crowded the northern part
of the city.[6]

For Salvado and other Catholics, this was not an
unwelcome development. The Roman Catholic Church
soon established a diocese in Liverpool—one of the few
in Britain—to minister to the city's Catholics. Even the
established agricultural and trading elite of Liverpool,
mostly Anglican, came to see this as a welcome presence,
a potential cork on the increasing crime and lawlessness
in parts of the city. So it was in Liverpool that Conaci
and Dirimera were introduced to Irish monks and priests.
Hardened men, they still had a playful sense of humour,
and made the boys laugh with small jibes. In church,
Conaci and Dirimera probably saw a harp being played

for the first time. They would have watched entranced as a monk's fingers plucked at its strings and then his palms smothered their ringing as they pushed flat against their reverberation. In the hollow of the church, the chords would echo and rise above the congregation, and for many hours afterward they rang in the ears of boys, who were ever-receptive to new sounds.

⌒

Today Liverpool remains a noisy city and its inhabitants are renowned for speaking their minds and being 'in your face'. In London and southern England, people talk about Liverpudlians with the amused tolerance that they might speak about children— suggesting their manners might be awful but also quaint and endearing.

Along its main street leading down to the docks, the shops open up into a pedestrian path. Commerce sprawls into the street and people bellow greetings at those a few feet away. The docks, gentrified now, are still busy with all kinds of people promenading. Liverpool's three grand old buildings, known as the three graces, include the domed Customs House. Other buildings that Conaci and Dirimera would have walked the floors of are gone. For Liverpool has been a centre of trouble ever since the 1800s. Having endured the wealth and the uprisings of the Industrial Revolution, much of it was later destroyed by war.

A key reminder of this destruction is St Luke's church, on the corner of Leece and Berry streets in the city's centre. When Conaci and Dirimera visited the city it was just fifteen years old. Its square tower and Gothic-style walls rise high, and its stones are carved with ornate patterns around the pointed arches of windows and doorways. A newspaper article of the time described St Luke's as it was when Conaci and Dirimera saw it: 'The entire inside has a most superb effect. The upper parts of the windows are decorated with stained glass ... the ceiling is richly ornamented and when viewed from the east end of the chancel offers an uncommonly grand coup d'oeil.'[7]

The ceiling, the window glass and the doors are now gone— St Luke's church was left gutted after it was hit by a bomb on 5 May 1941. Instead of rebuilding after the bombing, Liverpool's authorities decided it was better left as a reminder of what was lost in war.

When Conaci and Dirimera visited Liverpool, the city, like the British Empire, would have seemed so strong. It controlled not just rocks and mortar like these but trade, finance, the lives of thousands of workers and the immigration of millions more. I imagine this church as they must have seen it—its stone floor beneath, a roof above, the enclosed space suggesting shelter. There are some ruins that foster nostalgia for what they once looked like. St Luke's shell is a reminder of the fragility of power, civilisation and people themselves.

In contrast, Liverpool's main Catholic church, the Metropolitan Roman Catholic Cathedral of Christ the King, has large windows filled with more coloured glass than any church in Europe. A futuristic building, its design was determined by competition in the 1960s. It is circular with a domed roof rising to a column, the Lantern Tower, spiked with points like a crown that reach for the sky. Popularly, Liverpudlians call it The Wigwam, due to its resemblance to a Native American tepee.

When Conaci and Dirimera visited Liverpool, standing on the site of this cathedral was the largest workhouse in England—filled with the poor, who worked day in and day out for a mere ration of bread to feed themselves and their children.

⌒

After a short stay with the Catholic priests of Liverpool, Salvado and the boys made their way by ship to Dublin Bay. Alighting at the mouth of the Liffey River, they caught a horse-drawn carriage up into the city of Dublin. They sat and swayed alongside travelling members of the British upper classes, who were making their way into the provincial capital.

Coming from the south side of the city, their carriage passed the wide, round tower of Dublin Castle on the ridge overlooking the river, and the pointed spires of the Protestant Christ Church Cathedral. They passed the newly built university of Trinity College, where by law a copy of every book published in Great Britain and Ireland must be received and housed.

The central streets of Dublin were wide, with plenty of room for carriages to park, and they were flat, creating easy access across most of the city, along with the sturdy bridges that crossed the Liffey. The plain Victorian buildings sat beside new public buildings such as the domed Customs House. In its architecture, Dublin appeared much like Liverpool. In fact 'dubh-linn' in Gaelic means 'black pool', and the abundance of Irish accents in both cities must have made them appear similar to Conaci and Dirimera.

The key differences, of course, were things not seen. The poor in Dublin's streets looked as destitute as those in other cities, but their poverty was almost entirely caused not by industrialisation but by the potato famine. Many of the ragged in Dublin had given up hope of work and were seeking a way to emigrate—emptying the city and forming a great wave of migration to Britain and North America. An estimated one million people had left Ireland over the previous five years alone, and another million had died due to the famine.

The second unseen misery of Dublin was related to the lack of British action over the potato famine. This in turn had aggravated the long-troubled relationship of the Irish with the centre of power in London. In 1801 the Act of Union merged the parliaments of Dublin and London and created the United Kingdom of Great Britain and Ireland, known to most as Britain. Daniel O'Connell became known for his speeches against the Act of the Union, and in the 1820s he brought together Catholic organisations seeking to end discrimination against them. His campaign was funded by these Catholics, at a rate of a penny a month each, and O'Connell became a British parliamentry member.

Just twenty years before Conaci and Dirimera arrived in Dublin, the Emancipation Act enabled Catholics and followers of other religions to hold public office. In 1841 O'Connell became the first Catholic Lord Mayor of Dublin since the time of King James II in the 1600s. However, the desire for Irish freedom did not abate. Opposition to the Act of the Union revived in the 1840s, in a movement called Young Ireland, a newspaper called the *Nation* and mass demonstrations known as 'monster meetings'.

When Conaci and Dirimera visited in 1849, Ireland was seeking better times—an end to hunger, political subjugation, religious intolerance and economic dependency. The streets of Dublin might have seemed like those of any other British city, but the Irish had not yet wiped poverty and politics from their eyes to see their own future.

It is difficult to describe the religious passion of the Irish that Conaci and Dirimera would have sensed in Dublin at that time. There, more than anywhere else in the British Empire, religion became a political force. The British had done themselves no favours by levying tithes to support the Anglican Church from Irish peasants, and by banning those who followed other faiths from taking official roles on a local and national level. This suppression only bolstered support for Catholicism from the Irish peasantry and upper classes alike. By the 1840s the Catholic Church embodied the Irish people's sense of spirituality, politics and identity.

This story can be seen in Dublin's many statues. Each time I visit, the city seems to have more and more—a visitor can hardly walk through the streets without bumping into another statue recently erected to commemorate someone famous or ordinary, as befitting the mood of the City Council.

It was Victorian England that started this trend for monuments. When Conaci and Dirimera visited Dublin, they would have seen a huge column topped with a life-sized statue of Admiral Lord Nelson rising above the city's main thoroughfare, Sackville Street. Built in 1808 to commemorate the victorious Battle of Trafalgar against the Spanish and French fleets, in which Nelson lost his life, it was one of numerous statues erected in Dublin as symbols of British power. For the Green Isle had already rebelled numerous times—most recently in 1798, 1803, and in an insurrection by the Young Ireland group in 1848. The British elite of Dublin were still nervous over revolutionary activity across Europe when Salvado and the boys came to stay.

Now, Nelson's Pillar is gone, blown up by the Irish Revolutionary Army on 8 March 1966. Instead, an Irish leader stands on this street. At the base of the monument four angels represent the four provinces of Ireland. A few angels carry bullet holes, from struggles between British troops and Irish insurgents. On his own column, on his own street, which is no longer called

Sackville Street, Daniel O'Connell wears a cape and juts out his stomach like a proud pigeon. It is easy to see him as a political figure, but he is just as much a religious one. O'Connell's body is buried in Dublin's Glasnevin cemetery, established due to his own lobbying—after he saw a Catholic funeral interrupted by a Protestant minister—as a cemetery where people of all religions could be buried in peace. But his heart is in Rome, as he wrote in his will: 'My body to Ireland, my heart to Rome, my soul to heaven'.

While Salvado did not comment in his memoirs on O'Connell, probably for fear of arousing anxiety among Anglican readers in Perth, I wonder what side he would have taken on The Irish Question. Much of the Catholic Church supported O'Connell personally, if not the Irish independence movement generally. After O'Connell's death in 1847, Pope Pius IX gave instructions for a commemoration service in Rome, and in the funeral oration Father Ventura commented on O'Connell's last request:

> *He loves his country and therefore he leaves it to his body, he loves still more the Church and hence he bequeaths to it his heart; and still more he loves God, and therefore confides to Him his soul! Let us profit then, of this great lesson afforded by a man so great—a man who has done such good service to the Church, to his country and to humanity.*[8]

The passion for church, country and humanity is surely one that would have appealed to Salvado, but Ireland and Australia presented the monk with some difficult questions. Salvado had always been closely aligned to the monarchies of Europe, as these had upheld church power, but in the colonies of Ireland and Australia the interests of the common will of the people and of his church were often considered by the monarch, then Queen Victoria, only as an afterthought.

In Ireland the statues tell the story of the country's emancipation. Immediately before and in years following Irish independence, most of the English statues were removed, either officially by consent or unofficially by bombs. One that was carried out of Dublin before she could feel the tremor of dynamite was the statue of Queen Victoria. James Joyce, whose statue on North Earl Street shows him walking with a cane, giving rise to the nickname 'the Prick with the Stick', referred to this statue of Queen Victoria as the 'Auld Bitch'. She once stood in front of Leinster House, site of the Irish Parliament, but was removed by the authorities in 1947.

The 'Auld Bitch' was left alone in a warehouse for years, until she was given to Sydney in 1987 and placed on a stone pedestal in front of the Queen Victoria Building. Instead of looking down on her Irish subjects, she now looks soberly and disapprovingly at Australians, the flesh on her cheeks and the bags under her eyes sagging heavily. She has large, manly hands, and somehow delicately grasps a spiked staff in one hand and a globe and cross in the other. The fabric of her dress has the deep folds of a stiff material, and over her right shoulder is a sash and across her left breast is a medallion. She wears a crown on her flat head, which the sun shines through, but the metal is too dark to give her a glow.

This portrait of her fleshy skin, empty eyes and large hands gives a sense of her real features and her masculine air. She oversaw the world's largest empire at the time, the transport of thousands of convicts to Australia, millions of her own people working themselves into early graves and the suppression of Indigenous cultures from Australia to Africa.

To add to the colonial air of the Sydney location, and perhaps to counter the ferocity of the statue of Queen Victoria, it is accompanied by a smaller statue of—of all things—her dog. In front of the dog is a piece of stone from the battlements of Blarney castle that people rub for luck, and a fountain in which to throw a coin for deaf and blind children. The dog is a small Scottish terrier called Islay, standing in a begging pose on its back legs. I cannot help but laugh at the thought of what Irish patriots such as O'Connell would think of this commemoration of Queen Victoria and her pet at the other end of the earth. The history Australia has selected to remember is a curious choice.

⌒

As there were many monks and nuns in the streets of Dublin, Salvado in his dark robes attracted little attention. The boys, however, were notable, as only a few Indian and African people had made it to Dublin through trade or slavery. But the trio was welcomed by the local congregations, most of whom had little contact with or experience of the missions. Father John Smyth, who took them in, had news from New Norcia and Rome to pass on to Salvado. A first instalment of land around the mission in Western Australia had been secured, but money was still needed for another two land purchases. Salvado decided to make his way to Lyon to explain to the Council for the Propagation of the Faith why such funds should be forthcoming.

When they arrived again in England, after the journey by steamship across the strait, Salvado took the boys to the train station. The engine at the front of the train was clouded in smoke and became unbearably hot as the coal-fires were stoked and fuelled ready for departure. Carriages trailed behind this powerhouse—elegant covered carriages with white linen and butlers for first-class passengers, followed by the many plainer second-class carriages, then the trays on wheels, open to the wind and sky, in which third-class passengers stood and were covered in smoke and soot, and finally those stacked with cargo.

Conaci and Dirimera had not seen a train before, let alone stepped inside a carriage. The railway had been opened only five years earlier, and many of the passengers were similarly uninitiated and nervous. They crowded out the second-class cabin, which the boys had boarded—most people travelled in this class. When the train's whistle blew, their journey began, and they were soon travelling at about 70 kilometres an hour, which seemed astonishingly fast to Conaci and Dirimera. The boys were thrilled to feel the rattle of the wheels beneath them and to see the countryside pass by their windows with such speed. It was much more exciting than the slow horse-drawn carriages, or rocking on the waves in a boat or even cutting through the water in a steam-powered ship. 'Why not bring this kind of fire to Australia so we can go backwards and forwards between the Mission and Perth?' they asked Salvado.[9] For in Western Australia all travel was by horse or ship. After the train journey of less than twenty-four hours, the boys arrived in the huge mass that made up the city of London.

As soon as they stepped off the train and walked through the station into the light, Conaci and Dirimera must have known they were in another world entirely. Crowds of children with tattered clothing and smears of mud on their bodies surrounded Salvado. 'We're hungry, sir, can you help us?' 'Where are you from?' 'Sir, do you have any money?' When Dirimera looked down at the heads below him, he saw crawling insects in their hair. Some had runny noses and some sported bellies made round from hunger. The monk swung his bag around to clear a space for them in the crowd of Charles Dickens's children: the 'ragged, wretched, filthy, and forlorn' who filled his pages with as much energy as they crowded the streets. Conaci and Dirimera clutched at the monk's robes and they advanced with determination to a horse-drawn carriage. By the time the trio had walked those few metres, London had already overwhelmed them.

Simply put, in the 1800s London was the centre of everything. It was the largest urban area in the world. When Conaci and Dirimera climbed the flights of stairs to the room in which they stayed and looked out the window, the city's white, grey and red-brick buildings stretched on far beyond their horizon. Solitude was almost impossible to find in the mass of terraced buildings with barely a gap in which to fit streets. On these busy thoroughfares horses and horse-drawn carriages clopped through the city at all times of the day and night. An estimated thousand vehicles an hour passed over London Bridge each day.

The population of London had tripled in just fifty years and there were 2.5 million people in this city from all over Britain and its empire. Crammed together were some of the world's richest and poorest people, side by side in many areas. Even the Palace of Westminster was surrounded by some of the city's worst slums. At night London made a din, and slums operated in a world unto themselves—a harsh environment where people physically fought each other for basic necessities such as running water. Squatters stripped old houses of anything that could be sold, even the doors and their hinges and the panes of glass from the windows. The destitute and homeless slept in these empty shells, and those who could afford accommodation split their rent with as many people as floor space would allow.

Even inside the sanctuary of the guest room where they slept, the boys must have smelt London. It was a stench that could not be shut out. Most suburbs were built without sewage systems, and the scent of animal and human excrement filled the air. That very year, the Thames was described as a 'black fetid stream' and traffic on Fleet Street was blocked because the sewer urgently needed to be reconstructed at a deeper level. Even the rain was tainted, wrote Dickens:

> In the country, the rain would have developed a thousand fresh scents and every drop would have had its bright association with some beautiful form of growth or life. In the city, it developed only foul stale smells and was a sickly, lukewarm, dirt-stained, wretched addition to the gutters.[10]

The next day, Conaci and Dirimera would have passed through the slums of London with Salvado in order to reach the residence where the Secretary of the Colony of Western Australia, their shipboard companion Dr Madden, was staying. It was a tour of need, want and resourcefulness. Pockmarked women lined up to use the baker's oven after he had done his morning bake for paying customers, just to bake a small piece of dough. Markets filled with carcasses hanging in the air, newly slaughtered animals of all sorts dripping blood and staining the dust red. Cows were crammed into tiny sheds where there was no room for the sorry creatures to turn around, let alone think of escape, and they bellowed in distress. Women wiped the red blood of bullocks, painted on by dodgy market sellers, off the grey, rotting scales of fish, and creating an uproar over what was a common deceit. Children waded into the smelly Thames in search of saleable junk, and collected dog turds from the pavement in hessian sacks to sell to the leather tanners on the south bank, opposite the imposing Tower of London. Men in tailcoats nervously glanced at their pocket-watches, fortunately attached to their clothes by long gold or silver chains to deter thieves, before scurrying away from ever-present beggars.

When visiting the clergy of London, Conaci and Dirimera may have visited one of the soup kitchens that sprang up to help this struggling mass of people. One kitchen in Farringdon Street fed 8000–10 000 people daily, and more than a million pounds was spent per year in such direct attempts to alleviate poverty—with little effect.[11]

Finally making their way through this human cacophony, they happily left behind Dickensian London and entered the white Georgian apartments of Victorian London. The rooms where Madden and his family stayed were colourful: lined with patterned wallpaper and the furniture clad in foreign prints. Tea was served in white china rimmed with painted roses and poured by quiet girls a little older than ten. Their eyes widened when they set down the tray before two black boys, but they said nothing. If Conaci had smiled at one, he would have given her a fright, making her hands shake as she scurried back to the kitchen.

Madden took it upon himself to introduce Salvado to the 'chief authorities of London'. Visiting some of the clergy and colonial elite with Salvado, Conaci and Dirimera mingled, but did not meld, with the swelling middle and still-powerful upper classes. These were the offspring of men and women in Jane Austen's novels. They owned land and property, were served by maids and servants, drank the finest imported teas and coffees and carried on polite conversation, all the while taking discreet glances at their reflections in the shimmer of glass mirrors and the brass and gold ornaments that lined their homes.

Conaci and Dirimera would have seen women in day dresses that stretched from their chins to the ground and carrying parasols and shawls, which were usually in Victorian purple or the rich swirling paisleys from the East. At night, they would have seen much more of these women: they wore dresses made from coloured satin with the necklines cut low and usually square, while their faces were dotted with rouge and their hair was piled high on their heads. These women spent their days out, decking themselves in the latest fashions, shopping in Knightsbridge and drinking tea and coffee brought from Fortnum and Mason in Piccadilly and Charles Harrod's grocery shop.

The men Salvado discussed politics with were dressed in white, fawn or pale grey trousers with a dark tail coat, or they wore 'frock coats' covering their thighs. If they were of a higher class, their heads were covered with a silk top hat. When they visited another's home, the woman of the house would cover the backs of the sofas and armchairs with a white lace-edged cloth called an 'anti-macassar' to protect the furniture against the reddish brown shiny Macassar oil that men used to style their hair. Some men, as they talked, twirled their moustaches into neat curves above their upper lip. They were as concerned about fashion as the women but they talked about the world at large—a world of war, commerce, discovery and new ideas.

London was an intellectual centre as well as one of commerce. Liberalism had taken hold and individual rights had been achieved, but with voting rights limited to male property owners. Entrepreneurial Londoners passionately argued for freer trade and less regulation of business in order to retain the empire's economic might and to expand their own personal wealth. However, these ideas were not unchallenged. A year before Salvado, Conaci and Dirimera arrived in London, the city published John Stuart Mill's *Principles of Political Economy* which, following on from Jeremy Bentham's idea that political decisions should seek the greatest happiness for the greatest number of people, argued for government intervention in the economy through taxes and laws to protect the common man's rights.

As Conaci and Dirimera passed through the dirty streets of London, Karl Marx was in the same city, writing his attack on free enterprise and call for communal ownership of property: *Das Kapital*. Men of wealth who kept up to date with political debates were gasping with horror as they read in the just-published *Communist Manifesto*: 'The proletarians have nothing to lose but their chains. They have a world to win.'

If the sights, smell and ideas of London were not enough for visitors like our trio, there were the churches. Conaci and Dirimera were probably taken to Westminster Abbey, where every English monarch from William the Conqueror to George II was buried. It was Salvado's favourite London church:

> ... an outstanding work of Anglo Saxon architecture, now an Anglican chapter house ... Here, with a good deal of surprise, we discovered a small statue of our founder, Saint Benedict, who seemed, by remaining there all this time, to be asserting his claims over those sacred walls.[12]

Many centuries earlier, the library and other parts had been a Benedictine monastery. In the 1400s the Benedictine monks had been wealthy London landowners. King Henry VIII gave them the lands for the Priory of Hurley, in return for Covent Garden (the monks' vegetable garden), Hyde Park and property in Westminster. However, Henry was always covetous of the monks' possessions and in January 1540 he dissolved the monastery altogether and the monks had to sign a deed of surrender. From then on, the Abbey became Protestant, except for a short time when Queen Mary I, a Catholic, restored the Benedictines in 1556. After her death four years later her Protestant half-sister, Elizabeth I, removed the monks, and the present Collegiate Church of St Peter, Westminster was established.[13]

It was Salvado's connections with the clergy that led to his most prominent presentation of 'the grand experiment' to the British elite. One evening Salvado was invited by Nicholas Cardinal Wiseman, Archbishop of Winchester, to present to a 'meeting of learned men' the story of his experience of the Aboriginal people. He took Conaci and Dirimera along to illustrate his case: the living success of 'the grand experiment'.

In a private sittingroom, Conaci and Dirimera sat beside Salvado as a letter from New South Wales was read aloud to the group. It gave what Salvado described as 'an unfavourable opinion of the natives', arguing that Aboriginal people were incapable of intellectual thought. Particularly, it said that they did not understand the benefits of civilisation or the rights of property. Conaci and Dirimera listened to this politely, as the 'learned men' stared at them. The boys waited for Salvado to speak on their behalf. When the letter was finished, Salvado stood before the group, with Conaci and Dirimera standing beside him holding hands, as the monk took his opportunity to reply to these allegations.

Salvado argued that the boys he had in his care were perfectly capable of normal intellectual development, and indeed in music and languages had excelled beyond many white boys of the same age. He stated that the Yuet people at New Norcia mission had welcomed with open arms the opportunity to have their children educated in Western civilisation, that their conduct was orderly and that their respect for the mission's ownership of sheep and other goods was laudable. Through stories about his life with the Yuet people, Salvado backed up his statements with real experience. He later wrote in his diary, 'Although my opinion was different from those expressed in the letter and held by a number of people at the meeting, I had the satisfaction of seeing the majority of the members come round to my views'.[14]

If Conaci and Dirimera spoke at such events, their words were not recorded in Salvado's memoirs. Doubtless they had learned the principle of Victorian England, which stipulated that children should be 'seen but not heard'. Children were for the most part to do what they were told and rarely to offer opinions. This is what makes the novels of Charles Dickens so interesting. They give us a glimpse of the life of children and the life of the poor—two worlds scarcely seen or paid attention to at the time. Dickens portrayed these faceless people as having desires and fears, and with laughter and words forever tumbling from their ill-educated mouths.

The various people Conaci and Dirimera met must have influenced them, even if it was only subtly. In London, perhaps for the first time, they saw Salvado challenged—by children in the streets, by the London elite over his views about Aboriginal people, and by members of his Church. They were exposed to the absolute worst of European civilisation in the city's slums. Perhaps they began to understand that hardship was not necessarily about race, as they were confronted with a new concept: class. Perhaps they saw that the power of the Catholic Church was not unlimited and was challenged by another key force: the British Crown. Perhaps they had some sense that Salvado himself was an oddity in the world—a man who was not part of the State, the military or the economy but sought a role just as consequential outside these main sources of influence in society.

After two weeks in the stinking, crowded streets of London, the city Dickens called a 'black shrill city combining the qualities of a smoky house and a scolding wife',[15] the trio left for the College of Douai, near Reading. They were welcomed by the English Benedictines and given shelter overnight before heading out to the shores of the English Channel. There, they boarded a steamship bound for France.

Europe was just a grey blur of land on the horizon as the steamship chugged away through the dark sea. Conaci and Dirimera listened to the passengers. The boys were puzzled at the murmurs of excitement of the Europeans as they released their native tongues again in preparation for their return to a diverse and divided continent.

France

It was spring in Paris. The buds on the branches of oak and birch trees lining the city's streets opened out into soft, wet, lime green leaves. Bulbs spurted long stalks of tulips, crocuses and lilies in flowerpots on windowsills and in small urban gardens. Roses bloomed in their beds around the city's palaces. The sun, still gentle, cast a yellow light on the city's white and grey buildings, and the domes of its churches shone.

The city bloomed, yet Paris was at war. The moist air smelt of smoke and gunpowder. The golden walls of the houses and shops shook with the boom of gunfire. Bodies of men, common workers dressed in their white summer shirts and dark trousers, lay in the streets bleeding. Women peered from behind curtains at the chaos outside their doors. When Conaci and Dirimera looked out the window of their horse-drawn carriage, they saw the flanks of horses, the boots of soldiers pressing into their sides, their guns rattling as the army raced past in search of revolutionaries.

Just a year before the trio arrived in Paris, France had had its revolution and became a republic. Workers seeking the vote and political reform, many now branded as socialists, had joined the middle-class republicans seeking the vote for property owners and the advancement of commerce. Together these groups had risen in defiance of the French king, after his troops shot and killed people at an open-air meeting discussing the option of a republic. Thousands of Parisians had marched the streets crying 'Down with Louis Philippe!' They won, and the man who had famously said, 'There will be no reform. I do not wish it', fled in fright.

However, the flowering of newly freed France was soon thwarted by fighting between socialists and republicans.[1] The army of the newly elected government was forcing workers out of Paris when Conaci and Dirimera arrived in 1849.

When they saw a group of men run away and shouting at each other, followed by a division of soldiers, Conaci and Dirimera asked Salvado to explain what was the cause of this commotion. Salvado pointed at the fleeing workers and told the boys that these men were 'bad' and that the soldiers had to fire on them if they would not 'be good'. Conaci crinkled his face in confusion. 'But I see that the other men have rifles too', he said. 'Who will win?'[2]

Salvado replied, 'There are only a few of the bad men and so the soldiers will win'.[2] Conaci thought for a few minutes as the soldiers dashed past. When their footsteps were just a patter in the distance, he looked at Salvado. Dressed in his black robes, the monk appeared to Conaci as shorter than the long, gangly French, but he puzzled at Salvado's easy acceptance of his position as a bystander to this battle.

'Why don't you go between the soldiers and the bad men, take all their weapons away and lock them up in this house', Conaci asked, gesturing to a tall Parisian apartment building, 'so they will stop fighting, and the two of us will help you'.

'Because, this is not my country and I don't know anyone here', Salvado responded simply.

Conaci became agitated:

> That doesn't matter. You don't belong to my country either and you didn't know the natives but when they were getting ready to fight or had already started, you went in among them, took their gidjis [spears] shut them up in the Mission house and it was all over. Why don't you do the same here?[3]

Salvado said nothing to the insistent boy. He looked into his alarmed face, and words would not come into his mouth to reply. As he wrote in his diary:

> This argument, which was so much to the point and so unexpected from a boy who eight months before was

wandering naked in the bush and was as uncivilised as only a native can be, left me bereft of a satisfactory reply. I did not want to tell him that in a case like this it was easier to get good results from the natives than from those who boasted that they had reached the acme of civilisation.[4]

As he looked at Salvado, waiting for a reply, Conaci was perhaps recognising that his father-figure was indeed human.

The city was ravaged by disease and disruption. Many people died of cholera and others had nowhere to sleep, giving the elegant city a human smear that could not have escaped the boys' attention. For the first few days they saw only a little of this, as they were boarded up in apartments and churches, but a few days after their arrival, when the worst of the fighting had subsided, Salvado took them for a walk around the city's promenades along the River Seine. Conaci and Dirimera played games with each other while Salvado read from a book in the warm sun.

As the boys played, a French woman came over to them. Dressed in cotton shot with silk, she was very elegant. She bent over slightly and in soft French greeted them, asking where they were from. Conaci and Dirimera could not understand a word of it—only that the tone was friendly. Dirimera ran over to Salvado, interrupting his reading, 'There is a lady there who wants to say something to us, but, poor woman she does not know how to speak! Come and see if you can understand her.'

Salvado looked behind Dirimera at Conaci and the French woman, who had walked over to greet Salvado. He stood and addressed her in formal French. When he told her of what Dirimera had said, she did not laugh but let out a quick breath and a smile. The monk and the lady talked about the Aboriginal people of Australia, and about Conaci and Dirimera's education in particular.

She asked whether she could do anything to help further the boys' introduction to Europe. Salvado looked at Conaci and Dirimera, smiling politely at the woman who could not speak. Their trousers were patched and worn and, compared to the perfectly suited French boys around them, they could not help but look poor. Salvado asked if she might be so kind as to tell him, a clueless monk, where he could purchase clothing for the boys 'as cheaply as possible'. The lady replied, 'La Belle Jardinière'. Salvado took his notebook out from the long pocket of his robes to write down the shop's name. 'Don't bother writing it down, let me take you there', the woman said. She beckoned her maid and they crossed the garden, out into the shops of Paris.

Conaci and Dirimera laughed at each other in their new trousers, shirts and frock coats. Female shop assistants fussed around the two boys, fitting them correctly and teaching them how to fasten the big coat buttons. Salvado and the lady sat on a sofa discussing fashion and other matters.

When the boys were outfitted, Salvado stood to pay the bill, only to be told it had been taken care of. The lady smiled at Salvado and the boys, flushed from the excitement of their new clothes. Salvado asked for her name, so he could thank her properly. She shook her head and in a whisper to Salvado alone said, 'Pray for me'.

The next day Salvado and the boys left Paris. They travelled through the Rhône valley and its plantations of mulberry trees, where the locals picked out silk just spun by silkworms in the green folds of leaves. They passed fields of vines, the grapes green and getting ready to ripen in the early spring.

Arriving at Lyon, Conaci and Dirimera were impressed with how light and sunny the city appeared. Lyon's Roman name, Lugdunum, means 'hill of light' or 'hill of the crows'. It was reportedly founded as a Roman colony in 43 BC by Munatius Plancus, Caesar's lieutenant, who named it after the Celtic sun god, Lugh. On top of the Fouvière Hill are the Roman ruins of an amphitheatre, temple and public baths. Lyon sprang up on the side of that same hill, its alleys winding towards the Saône and Rhône rivers, which ran into each other. Across the river from this hill, new Lyon sat more square and straight-laced, with smoky silk mills and other factories.

The architecture of Lyon was similar to that of Paris but with more of an Italian influence—many buildings painted a soft yellow and giving off a Mediterranean glow. Many of the walkways in the old town were covered, forming a web of alleys, while the new town stretched out openly to the sun. As they passed through the city, Conaci and Dirimera saw stores filled with coloured silk— green, violet, pink, red, yellow, auburn, blue, black and more colours shone in the sun. They were woven into soft, light silk, rich jacquard prints and dense raw silk. King Louis XI had decided in the fifteenth century to establish Lyon as a central manufacturer of gold and silk fabrics, and King François I later established by royal order financial incentives for the silk business to move to Lyon. A large community of Italians took advantage of the offer and serviced growing fashion centres across the border, such as Milan.

Proclaimed capital of the three Gauls in the first century, Lyon had always been a business centre, and Salvado was there on business. He had come to the second-largest city in France, capital of the Rhône–Alpes region and home of the Archbishop of France (known as the Primate of the Gauls), to secure support for New Norcia— both financial and political.

The Cathedral Saint-Jean, where the Primate of the Gauls had his home, was built in the twelfth and fifteenth centuries. Conaci and Dirimera may have stopped to listen to the church's astronomical clock, which chimes a hymn to St John as a rooster crows and carved angels herald the Annunciation.

Inside, the Romanesque and Gothic church has held funerals and marriages of France's elite, lighted by large stained-glass windows. The royal Bourbons left their mark in their chapel, which is adorned with medallions depicting the signs of the zodiac, the creation of the world and the life of St John. There, Salvado held a brief meeting with the clergy, and Conaci and Dirimera once again tried to make sense of the French language.

Out in the bright streets they followed Salvado to his next meeting, with the Society for the Propagation of the Faith. The society was started by a woman, who came 'to be a friend of Salvado's—Pauline Jaricot. Born in Lyon as the daughter of a rich trader, she became fascinated by the idea of foreign missions and for a time dreamed of becoming a missionary herself. But she was also drawn into the society of silk merchants, writing later, 'I dressed myself in all my finery, believing myself worthy of universal admiration and preening myself with the conceit of a peacock'.[5] When she heard a sermon, the subject of which was vanity, she made her confession, went home, burnt her romantic novels and songs and decided never again to look into a mirror. She began to visit the poor and dress as though poor, encouraged her brother to become a missionary and founded the Society for the Propagation of the Faith in 1822.

Its purpose was to raise funds for missionary work and it used her practice of approaching people individually for donations, each supporter getting ten more donors, and each of these ten more, so that the society grew in numbers rapidly. The method was far more successful than the usual collection boxes and the like, and the society soon spread to Ireland in 1840, Britain in 1850 and, after Jaricot's death in 1862, a branch was established in the United States in 1880. She was fifty years old when she met Conaci and Dirimera but is described even then as looking young. She had blurred vision, and the boys must have stood close for her to see them, maybe even to touch them. Pauline listened attentively to Salvado, paying every kindness to the two boys in his care and eventually confirming for the monk the funds he needed for New Norcia.

After this business was concluded, Salvado and the boys wandered around Lyon as the sun set. They passed the Abbey of Saint Martin d'Ainay, a Benedictine monastery built in Romanesque style many centuries earlier but now opened as a museum (today it stands as a fine arts museum). The terracotta roofs of the houses became brighter orange and the walls a softer cream in the light of the setting sun. The river, wide and blue, was only a murmur as the water ran, and the whole city had a peace about it, far removed from the turmoil of Paris.

Of course, being such a large industrial centre, Lyon was not always so tranquil. It too had problems with exploitation of labour and the suffering of the poor. In 1831 and 1834 the Canuts, as silk workers are known, revolted. Following the introduction of the jacquard loom, the price paid for a length of silk was halved. Attempts to regulate the price to protect increasingly indebted silk workers floundered, and manufacturers refused to agree to a minimum rate for custom work. By November 1831 tensions reached a head and the Canuts marched down the Montée de la Grande Côte with black flags, shouting, 'Live working or die fighting!' Guards shot at the crowd, killing three, and the Canuts barricaded themselves on the side of the hill. For three days the sun-filled streets of Lyon were a battleground, with the Canuts using knives, sticks and stones to defend themselves. Despite the death of around six hundred people the manufacturers maintained the freedom to set prices, and since then Lyon's workers had been regarded with suspicion.

By the time Conaci and Dirimera arrived, the fear of workers was such that even puppets were a source of controversy. The boys may have seen a street performance of the puppet Guignol, such was his popularity at the time. A poor silk worker, Guignol was the Everyman of Lyon. In appearance he was not dissimilar to England's Punch—with a large caricature face, a Gallic nose and a thin body. He had an ill-tempered wife, Madelon, and the neighbourhood drunk, Gnafron, for company. Guignol was frequently in trouble with the police for minor infractions of the law, but otherwise was hard working and moral. Performances were usually over-the-top comedy with a few off-the-cuff jokes and political remarks. Just a couple of years after Conaci and Dirimera's visit, the content of Guignol's performances led to a demand that all scripts be sent to the authorities for approval, and improvisation was banned. Napoleon III's authorities, in particular, were concerned that Guignol would lead the people of Lyon astray—into workers' organisations, dissent and political agitation.[6]

⌒

While Conaci would have been soaking up the new sensations and people in the city of light, Dirimera was increasingly feeling dark. In Lyon he became ill—feverish, tired and nauseous. It was the beginning of health problems that would trouble him for many years to come. Medical knowledge was not as it is today and many illnesses that are now easily identified were often put down to the climate or to the physiology of the sick person, rather than to a biological cause. In addition, many doctors—never having administered to a person who was not white—would have considered Dirimera to be substantially physically different from other patients. Frustratingly, his health problems were neither correctly identified nor treated and they simply ran their course through his body.

Salvado took Dirimera to a Lyonnais doctor who, in keeping with the theory of the times, told Salvado that the changeable spring air of Lyon was not good for him. The doctor's orders were to head south to warmer climes, which Dirimera's body was more used to. Salvado packed the boys' trunks and headed south by horse-drawn carriage

As I left Lyon to head south into Provence and towards the southern coast, I thought of Dirimera sitting by the window, feeling the breeze and smelling the scent wafted from what his blurred eyes could see—fields of vines dripping green and with dark grapes under the shade of their leaves, the violet stalks of lavender and dark twigs of rosemary becoming dry and pungent in the sun, lemons and oranges ripening on branches. Did he see the small villages perched on slopes, the cows and goats in the valleys? Or did he close his eyes and sleep in an attempt to conserve energy?

I imagined the discomfort of travelling when Dirimera was so ill, and Salvado tending to him with water and damp cloths. I thought of Conaci talking animatedly to Dirimera to keep him awake as the world passed by—about what he saw, about home, about anything to keep his friend distracted from his pain and nausea.

Even when surrounded by beauty and excitement, when you are sick there is nothing you want more than to be at home. Dirimera must have felt fear. He now knew he was in a land where the three of them were vulnerable to war and disease, and he did not have recourse to language or kin to protect himself. If he wondered why he had come to Europe, it was too late to turn back. It had been a long time since he had felt the warm skin of his mother, watched her walking off with her digging stick, the kangaroo skin slung over her back, her eyes in search of food. It had been months since Dirimera had felt the soft blow of air of a kiss from his father, watched him scratch his beard or listened to his patient teachings about the hunt and about the passing down of weapons from father to son. Now that his body was frail, the time apart must have seemed even longer. All Dirimera could do was wait until his condition improved and imagine that one day all this travel would be behind him and he would be home, sitting by a warm fire, listening to the language he knew was his.

⌒

Salvado, Conaci and Dirimera soon reached the warmer port of Marseilles. Like Lyon, the city had a suggestion of vigour in its people—so many revolutionaries from Marseilles had marched from the Rhine to Paris in 1792 that the 'Hymn of the Army of the Rhine' became known as 'La Marseillaise', the national anthem. The people of Marseilles were tanned, boisterous and Mediterranean, enlivening the stone buildings with noise and colour.

Conaci and Dirimera walked through the Arc de Triomphe de la Porte d'Aix, which marks the old entrance to the city. Above them the spire of the Romano-Byzantine Basilique Notre-Dame de la Garde looked down over the city like a watchtower. They reached their lodgings somewhere between these two points on the side of the hill, and Dirimera could feel the sea breeze from his bed at night.

For the next few days Salvado often had to carry Dirimera down the ancient road, La Canebière, to the sea. On the way, Dirimera would have seen old men, sailors and workers drinking pastis in the sun. He smelt its heady mix of alcohol, star anise, black and white peppercorns, cardamom, sage, nutmeg, cloves, cinnamon, liquorice and sugar. He saw women buying orange-flavoured cakes from the old Benedictine nunnery. He heard native Italian, as many Italians came and went from this key port into France.

Salvado lay Dirimera on the shore and sat with him while he caught the salty breeze and felt the summer sun on his sweaty skin. Dirimera smelt the seaweed, the fish from ships coming ashore, the hemp ropes being taken on board. He saw Conaci running to the shore after the gulls. He watched Salvado pray for him. In his fever it must have seemed as though he dreamed the stone city by the sea with so many forts, which were actually churches.

After a few days in Marseilles, Salvado bustled the boys onto a ship bound for the Kingdom of the Two Sicilies. That same ship was delivering dispatches to the Pope. Salvado was excited to hear that the French Army was returning to Rome to restore monarchical order. Like France, Italy had been rocked by rebellions the year before. The unrest had begun in Sicily and spread further, with people challenging the local aristocracies and calling for the unification of Italy as one nation. Nationalists had seized Rome from Pope Pius IX in late 1848, but he and aristocratic Italian rulers received aid and armies from Austria and France. They reversed many gains made by the revolutionaries until all that remained of the nationalist uprisings was a liberal constitution in Piedmont—in all the other kingdoms and in the Vatican the combined forces had managed to push the revolutionaries back. They had just restored control by the time Salvado, Conaci and Dirimera set sail for southern Italy on 27 June.[7]

Salvado thought this was 'reassuring news'—he feared that if the nationalists made progress, the Church's assets would be seized and the monasteries closed, as had happened in his youth in Spain. He had already lived through unrest in Spain, Italy and France, and he wanted the restoration of conservative order so that he could pursue further missionary activity in Europe and abroad. In addition, he wanted to see Conaci and Dirimera well protected by the sanctity and teaching of the Benedictines, and planned to place the boys in the monastery he had been schooled at—Badia di Cava de' Tirreni on the southern Italian coast.

On the ship, Dirimera's fever worsened, and he sweated, coughed and vomited repeatedly. As Salvado wrote, 'During this voyage the condition of young Dirimera had become much worse, so that if we had had to sail for any longer time, I should have perhaps lost him for good'.[8] Assured by all that Dirimera would be well suited to the southern European climate and would recover, Salvado looked hopefully towards the sails billowing and the bow cutting the waves as they sailed south into Italian waters.

Italy

Dirimera's red eyes looked with a hint of hope across the bay towards Naples. In the summer sun it was a blur of golden buildings stretching out over the curve of land in front of the indignantly silent grey volcano of Vesuvius. Dirimera could not wait to get off the ship that had made him feel so ill. Conaci too had acquired a nervous energy about him since Dirimera's health had become so perilous. Although Conaci was a confident boy he must have had a small tremor in his heart at the thought of losing his only connection with his tribe. If Dirimera's body failed him, Conaci would be left alone in this land of men who spoke like music and had dark eyes that could smile or frown.

As the trio went ashore, they were met by health inspectors. The Neapolitan authorities, in an attempt to control cholera, which had been particularly rampant in France, put Dirimera into quarantine for a week. Still very ill, he was able to rest and was tended by nuns. It must have reminded him of his first stay at the mission—once again he was interned in white sheets and tended by people wearing black and speaking a language he could not understand. He slept much of the time and slowly began to recover from his persistent fevers and nausea. Sometimes he woke in a sweat, confused about his whereabouts. At other times the fever made him dream all kinds of amalgamations from his past and his present—Europe and Australia.

Meanwhile, Salvado and Conaci met the noblemen of Naples. They climbed winding stone staircases, stood in the sun on tiled balconies overlooking the city, walked through rooms decked out with potted palms, gilded mirrors, chairs like thrones, and frescoes of gods, both Ancient Greek and Christian, on the ceiling.

At night, Salvado and Conaci dined at the finest tables, lit by candelabras and decorated with flowers. They ate meat of all kinds, fruits piled high on platters and giant fish from the Mediterranean. Conaci watched the men, dressed in tailcoats and often with moustaches, talking, consuming and posturing, knowing that they controlled people just as they controlled their dogs—skinny creatures with large noses and an impression that they had stumbled in from the streets to slip under the table as a shadowy reminder of reality.

Ruled by the King of the Two Sicilies at the time, Naples was a key port and centre of power. Salvado secured financial support and lodgings from two noblemen named in his diaries, Signor Leopoldo Galuzzo and Signor Antonio Paino. In their palaces, where they watched from wide windows the ships coming and going from the warm aqua seas, Conaci could imitate the sounds of people speaking Italian. But Dirimera was not there to listen with him or to talk to in their own language. If Conaci could have understood conversations around him, he would have quickly been introduced to Italian politics—of Church and State.

In a revolt the previous year, the prime minister of the Papal States had been assassinated and a key revolutionary leader, Giuseppe Mazzini, and other supporters declared a Roman republic. They broke down the ghetto walls that divided Rome, and encouraged Romans to take to the streets to celebrate the end of the theocracy.

The Pope had caused widespread alarm among the monarchs of Italy and their hangers-on when he fled to Gaeta, just south of Naples. Afflicted with epilepsy in his youth, the strength of Pope Pius IX had always been a source of concern. Although he came from a noble family, the Ferrettis, the future Pope was known for his interest in women and billiards as a youth. Originally he applied to become a Noble Guard, but was rejected due to his health problems and instead became a priest. He became known in Chile and Peru, where he travelled, and in Imola, near Bologna, where he served as a bishop. A surprise successor to the papacy when Pope Gregory XVI died in 1846, the initial days of Pius IX seemed to herald greater political liberty. He released political prisoners and reaffirmed sympathy for Italian nationalism—but later refused to join the war against Catholic Austria, which controlled most of northern Italy.

After being forced out of Rome, he returned with a harsher view of the revolutionaries, and reintroduced the ghetto for Jews. Although the ghetto walls were never rebuilt, he firmly established them in society and politics. He reacted so negatively to any sign of democracy, nationalism or equality that instead of Pio Nono (Pius the Ninth), some called him Pio No No for his willingness to say 'no' to any change. He went forth strengthening the Church's power, rebuilding control across Italy and creating many new dioceses—including Melbourne, Australia, in 1847.

Pius IX had only just re-established control of Rome when Salvado arranged an appointment with him at his hideout in Gaeta. The meeting was arranged through the diplomacy of Prince Sebastian, a member of the Spanish royal family who had moved to Naples during Spain's civil wars of the 1830s. He lived there under the protection of his brother-in-law, King Ferdinand II of the Two Sicilies. By the time this key meeting was arranged, Dirimera's week in quarantine and his fever had passed. He joined Conaci and Salvado on their final visit to their Neapolitan noble friends, leaving the austerity of the hospice for the rich but decaying rooms of a palace by the sea. After a drink and much discussion, the signors accompanied Salvado down to the shore, where he led the boys onto a ship that was taking the short journey south to Gaeta.

The green waters became calm and still as they entered the bay of Gaeta. The city stretched out along a long, sharp bend of coast covered in Italian buildings painted soft yellow, pink and red in Baroque touches. An occasional palm or orange tree poked out of the gardens of houses of the landed and trading elite who lived in the city. The small hill behind the city's cobbled streets was capped with an unassuming fort, Castello Angioino—a tower built with round cobblestones attached, without sophistication, to a large rectangular building with few windows. As their ship swung around to head into the port, Conaci and Dirimera looked at the coast on the other side of the bay and saw wild hills covered in green and only a few scattered villages, marked by the red drops of terracotta roofs on the land's slope.

Rowing to shore, Salvado pointed out the spire of the twelfth-century cathedral, painted a papal red in parts. Its tower was topped by four corner columns that seemingly held up a piece of stone cut into a pendant. Approaching the cathedral itself, Conaci and Dirimera noted the geometric mosaics of blue, green and white tiles all around the spire. As they entered, they saw ancient Roman lions protruding from its walls as a reminder of the city's regal and mythical stature. In the *Aeneid* (VII, 2), Virgil told the legend of Cajeta, Aeneas's nursing mother, who died here and was buried in the sands of Gaeta. Another theory about the city's name is that it came from the Greek word 'kaiatas', meaning cave. Recently it had been a hiding place for both the King of the Two Sicilies and the Pope. Its narrow alleys shaded people from the view of those at sea, and entering the cathedral was like going underground.

As they opened its heavy doors and walked the passage, Roman carvings on the wall showed men being eaten by chimeras: mythical creatures with the heads of lions, wings of birds and long bodies of eels. Inside it was like night, and candles revealed some of the gold leaf on the walls. This dense and dark space offered solace for men and women of Gaeta weary of the heat, and for foreigners of the busy port. Here Salvado said Mass with the other priests, and Conaci and Dirimera were lost in the drone of prayer.

The morning they arrived in Gaeta, 29 July, Salvado, Conaci and Dirimera went to a palace where the Pope was staying. On the way, through the streets of narrow coffee shops, carpets hanging from balconies, chickens in cages and people cramming space with noise and sweat, Salvado schooled Conaci and Dirimera in the etiquette of meeting the Pope. They were to step forward and kiss the Pope's hand if offered. They were not to speak unless spoken to. They were to bow their heads and not stare.

Salvado told them they were about to meet the most holy man in the whole world, and with his blessing they would become the holiest Aboriginal men in Australia. It was a great day and the short Spaniard had a jaunt in his step as he talked to the boys in both broken English and Yuet language to make sure they understood.

Papal Guards lined the hallways as the trio was ushered through the Pope's residence. With their knives at their sides and their rifles slung over their shoulders, the guards were a reminder of the power of the Church and of its enemies. After a winding journey into the heart of the palace, a door opened to a spacious, bare room at the end of which was a solitary throne in which sat His Holiness.

Although a relatively young 56-year-old, Pope Pius IX maintained an authoritative air. His white robes flowed over his knees and down to his feet as he sat in a large throne made higher by the stone step on which it was placed. His greying soft curls framed a face that was thin, with protruding and intense eyes from which there was no release.

Salvado went forward and knelt before the Pope, kissing his hand while thanking him for the kindness he had bestowed on the mission and its Aboriginal subjects. The Pope nodded in reply and asked what the two black boys were carrying. Salvado replied:

Holy Father, each one of these white linen bags contains a monastic habit and as these two lads are going to become the first Benedictines of Australia, indeed, of a whole fifth of the whole world, I humbly ask you to let them have the great honour of receiving the habit from your hands.[1]

'I am only too happy to do so', Pius IX replied, taking the habit from Dirimera. Kneeling before the Pope, Dirimera was wrapped in the dark cloth and blessed as Pius IX touched a light finger to the boy's shoulders and then asked his name. 'John Baptist', said Salvado. 'Well, from henceforth he will have the name of Joannes Maria', said Pius IX. Maria was the Pope's own baptismal name.

He then turned his beady eyes to Conaci, who stepped forward and offered the Pope the cloak. As he took it, Conaci kneeled as Dirimera had done, hands clasped together in prayer, as the cloak was put over his head. When told his name was Francis Xavier, the Pope commented that Conaci should retain this name: 'Australia needs a second Francis Xavier; may the Lord bless this boy and make him into one!' As they made their way to leave, the Pope gave each boy a silver crucifix to hang around their necks and Salvado a set of rosary beads.[2] Conaci and Dirimera walked out into the glaring sun and Mediterranean shore as the first two black Benedictines to be blessed by the Pope.

When they reached the Baroque palace of Signor Dabunno, where Salvado had been invited to stay, he received a note stating that King Ferdinand II of the Two Sicilies had heard that the monk and his Australian

Benedictines were in Gaeta, and requesting their company. The king's constitution was suited to such genteel ceremonies, but circumstances had drawn him into the depths of politics, where he barely kept afloat. Becoming king when he was just twenty, he married Maria Christina of the royal house of Savoy in his early twenties, then an Austrian princess, Maria Theresa, when in his late twenties.

That same year an outbreak of cholera and resentment of royal rule had led to a revolt in Sicily. A group known as La Giovine Italia (Young Italy) tried to capitalise on this unrest and organise a general uprising but, fortunately for the king, its success was limited. When the king condemned the Bandiera Brothers, two siblings who had led a small uprising in his kingdom, encouraged by Mazzini, they shouted 'Viva L'Italia' as they were executed. This tale only popularised the cause, and the harsh sentences soon dispelled any idea that the king's reported gentle nature would translate into a more liberal outlook.

When a dispute arose in 1848 over the nature of an oath taken by members of the chamber of deputies, the king regretted having granted a constitution. After fighting in Naples, the short-lived national parliament was dissolved on 13 March 1849. In retaliation for the trouble caused by revolutionaries, the king ordered that the chief cities of Sicily be bombed, earning him the title of King Bomba. By the time Conaci, Dirimera and Salvado were to make the king's acquaintance, British authorities estimated there were thousands of political prisoners in the gaols of southern Italy.

Giuseppe Tomasi di Lampedusa, a Sicilian nobleman who was the Duke of Palma and Prince of Lampedusa, wrote a portrait, believed to be based on King Ferdinand II, in his masterpiece, *The Leopard*. It gives an impression of what Conaci and Dirimera might have expected from a meeting with His Royal Highness. Tomasi di Lampedusa describes the journey of nobleman Salina to the king's court:

They moved through innumerable rooms of superb architecture and revolting décor (just like the Bourbon monastery itself), plunged into dirty passages and up ill-kept stairs and finally emerged in an anti-chamber filled with waiting people: the closed faces of police spies, the avid faces of petitioners. The chamberlain apologised, pushed through this mob and led him towards another ante-chamber reserved for members of the Court; a little blue and silver room of the period of Charles III. After a short wait, a lackey tapped at the door and they were admitted into the August Presence.

The private study was small and consciously simple; on the white-washed walls hung a portrait of King Francis I and one, with an acid, ill-tempered expression, of the reigning Queen; above the mantelpiece was a Madonna by Andrea del Sarto looking astounded at finding herself in the company of coloured lithographs representing obscure

Neapolitan saints and sanctuaries; on a side table stood a wax statuette of the Child Jesus with a votive light before it; and the modest desk was heaped with papers, white, yellow and blue; the whole administration of the kingdom here attained its final phase, that of signature by His Majesty (D.G.)

Behind this paper barrier was the King. He was already standing so as not to be seen getting up; the King with his pallid heavy face between fairish side-whiskers, with his rough cloth military jacket under which burst a purple cataract of trousers. He gave a step forward with his right hand out and bent for the hand-kiss which he would then refuse.

'Well, Salina, blessings on you!' His Neapolitan accent was far stronger than the chamberlain's.[3]

The king's court was in a flurry about the meeting of His Majesty and the exotic black Benedictines. Salvado led the boys through a gaggle of soldiers dressed in royal uniforms with padded shoulders, ladies in their best dresses with wide hooped skirts, merchants with new tailored jackets, priests in dark robes and pointed hats—all making gasps of greetings at one another. Salvado took the hands of Conaci and Dirimera and weaved through the throng to the centre of attention. As they approached, the assembled people gave way to a group of men—the king's advisers and guards—all dressed as though ready for war. The room hushed and watched. 'The devout and large hearted King welcomed us with the kindness that comes so naturally to him', Salvado reported. He immediately began talking over with the king the story of the mission and its success in making progress with the local Aboriginal people, in a loud voice so as to be heard by the elite of southern Italy.

While Salvado talked with the king and his court, Dirimera was pondering the flanks of soldiers who lined every corridor leading to the room where the king and queen were enthroned. He interrupted Salvado to ask if the king was the father of all those soldiers.[4] Salvado, without the time to explain fully, said this was true. Dirimera nodded and replied, 'In that case he must be a very brave and good man, at least that is the way it seems!'

'That is the way it seems and that is the way it is', said Salvado. The king was curious about this exchange in English and wanted to know what had been said about him. Salvado explained in Italian, and the king 'could not help smiling at these words of praise that were so ingenious and well deserved'.

At the same time, Conaci was fascinated by the queen, who had unfolded a fan made of stiff lace and was using it to cool herself in the heat of the midday sun, which penetrated even the palace's walls and brought drops of sweat to the napes of the men's necks. He took a few steps forward and without a word took the fan, as Salvado describes it, 'without any rudeness from her hands and tried it out on both himself and the Queen'. She was charmed, writes Salvado, 'She understood his innocence and not only overlooked his boldness but gave each boy a fan, which brought them much pleasure'.

Conaci clearly would have enjoyed playing with the queen, but the appointment with the king was ushered to an end by his minders. As a parting gift the king gave Conaci and Dirimera a gold medal with an image of the Virgin on it. He also offered to be responsible for the education and furnishing of rooms for the boys at the monastery in Cava, and invited Salvado to pay him a visit each evening during their week-long stay in Gaeta. The two 'black Benedictines' and Salvado became celebrities, each night meeting another curious noble who had heard about the king's new subjects and threw his weight behind 'the grand experiment'. For Conaci and Dirimera the festivity and wealth of the royal circuit must have seemed light and amusing compared to the dark monastery they were to visit next.

⌣

At first concrete and unassuming, Gaeta offers glimpses of its former self in the smiling arc of its old town, capped by the fort. Quiet even in the height of the summer tourist season, which leaves Gaeta itself untouched, it leaves no particular impression on the odd lost tourist—possibly because, like many port cities, it no longer has a sense of self-importance.

Father Rosendo Salvado, the Benedictine missionary who befriended two Nyungar boys in the Australian bush and took them to Europe, poses here in his work clothes. This photograph was probably taken during a visit to Rome in the early 1850s.

(Courtesy Benedictine Community of New Norcia Archive)

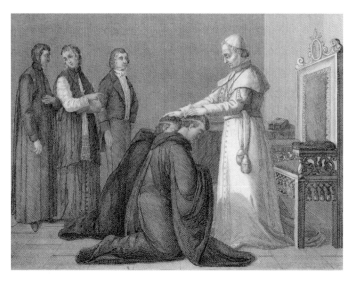

Father Rosendo Salvado and Father José Serra are blessed by Pope Gregory XVI before setting out to Australia in 1845. The two men met in a monastery at Santiago de Compostela in the north of politically tumultuous Spain, and encouraged each other to become missionaries. They founded the mission of New Norcia in Western Australia in 1846. (Engraving by Pablo Alaborn, circa 1851, commissioned by Father Rosendo Salvado in Italy, courtesy Benedictine Community of New Norcia Archive)

Fathers Salvado and Serra tend to the local Yuet people. The missionaries became known to the Yuet as able healers, and as mediators in their conflicts with white farmers. (Engraving by Pablo Alaborn, circa 1851, commissioned by Father Rosendo Salvado in Italy, courtesy Benedictine Community of New Norcia Archive)

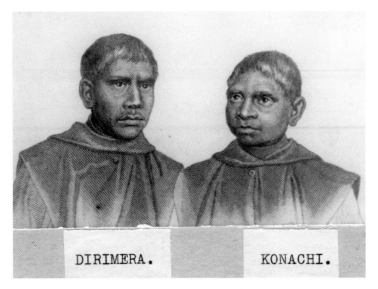

DIRIMERA.   **KONACHI.**

The only depiction we have of Conaci and Dirimera, this engraving was commissioned
by Salvado in Italy before he left the boys at the Badia di Cava de' Terreni monastery.
Dirimera (*left*), the elder of the two, is aged about twelve and Conaci, ill at this stage,
is about ten. (Engraving by Pablo Alaborn, circa 1851, courtesy Benedictine Community
of New Norcia Archive)

This engraving shows Dirimera receiving the dark robes of a monk from Pope Pius IX.
Conaci waits his turn, and Salvado, then in his early thirties, holds the dark cloth.
The meeting took place in Gaeta—tall ships and mountains can be seen through the
window—where the Pope had been forced to flee from Italy's rising revolutionaries.
(Engraving by Pablo Alaborn, circa 1851, commissioned by Father Rosendo Salvado in Italy,
courtesy Benedictine Community of New Norcia Archive)

The old town of Gaeta on the southern Italian coast appears today much as it would have when Conaci and Dirimera arrived in the 1849. Here they met both the Pope and the King of the Two Sicilies, and the king agreed to be their patron and help fund their studies at Badia di Cava de' Tirreni monastery.

The Badia di Cava de' Tirreni monastery stretches out along the mountainside. It was here that Salvado placed Conaci and Dirimera to complete their Western education. Established in 1011 and still operating as a monastery today, the grounds contain several churches, an underground grotto, a school and a large archive.

The exterior of Santo Paulo Basilica in Rome attached to which is Santo Paulo Fura le Mura, the monastery where Conaci stayed while ill. Santo Paulo is considered by many to be second only to the more famous Santo Pietro (St Peter's) in beauty and religious significance.

When the boys arrived in 1853, Santo Paulo Fura le Mura was shiny new—reconstruction had just been completed after a great fire in 1823 destroyed much of the old complex. This view is from the cloister into the courtyard.

New Norcia's Holy Trinity Abbey church was first erected in 1861. In 1908, the façade was rebuilt in this Spanish style, recalling the homeland of the mission's founders, Fathers Salvado and Serra. Benedictine missionaries also established several missions in the United States, notably California.

(Courtesy Lucas Ride)

New Norcia monastery as it looks today. Missionary work and the schooling of Aboriginal children ceased in the 1970s, and Australia's only monastic town is now a tourist attraction, a few hours' drive from Perth. (Courtesy Lucas Ride)

Nyungar boy Conaci was named after the black cockatoo, depicted here in a drawing by the author.

Stained glass windows at New Norcia monastery combine modern realism and Indigenous themes. In 2000 a small plaque was erected to recognise the many Aboriginal people who lived and died on the mission from its founding in 1846 until 1973. (Courtesy Lucas Ride)

The rundown city has the feeling of an old man who was once a well-travelled soldier and now sits on a verandah, thoughtfully, with only his eyes suggesting the stories he no longer can be bothered to recount. The city has long enjoyed a military presence, thanks to its strategic position as a port looking out to Naples, the island of Sardinia and the boot toe of Italy. The Romans recognised this with a strong presence in the city, and even today Gaeta's dialect retains the Latin neuter gender and sounds almost ancient. On Split mountain, so named because it is said to have split into three after the death of Christ, there are the remains of the first-century mausoleum of Roman general Lucius Munatius Plancus. In addition to its strategic place in the monarchies of Italy and the revolution, Gaeta was also a key port during both world wars and is currently a base for NATO.

Despite this role, Gaeta has been left to decline in economic stature and appearance, and few care where the palace of the King of the Two Sicilies may have been. After an assassination attempt in 1856 and France and Piedmont declaring war on Austria (which would eventually result in the end of his kingdom), the king died of natural causes on 22 May. He was succeeded by his son, Francis II, who was much less respected among his subjects than his father. In the film version of The Leopard, Burt Lancaster, playing the noble Prince Salina, shaves while his younger nephew, Tancredi, talks of his support for the revolutionaries. Salina argues that, as a nobleman, Tancredi should throw his support behind the king, to which Tancredi replies, 'If Ferdinand were still alive ... but little Francis? God bless him, but no!'

As Garibaldi's troops advanced in pursuit of the end of monarchies and the beginning of a free Italy, Gaeta became the last stronghold of the Bourbon royalty. They locked themselves into the fortress on the hill with twelve thousand scared soldiers, who eventually surrendered, along with King Francis, on 13 February 1861. Monarchical control had ended and the unification of Italy was complete.

Following this historic moment, Gaeta changed its allegiance and became known for its role in unification. The fort, which is probably where the king met Conaci and Dirimera, now bears no sign of his royal presence or that of his defeated son. Instead, a bronze plaque on a gatepost reads, 'Caserma Giuseppe Mazzini' (Fortress of Giuseppe Mazzini) in commemoration of the revolutionary nationalist leader who is second in fame only to Giuseppe Garibaldi. The king's fort is now a base for a government department regulating commerce and financial affairs. Yellow and black signs warn anyone approaching that the fort it is a 'zona militare', and it is fenced off to protect the interests of the Arma Financia, a department whose purpose remains vague to most Italians.

It is also possible that Conaci and Dirimera met the king in the walled, square stone barracks by the sea, which now sits forlornly beside a small park looking at the water. The building is covered in weeds growing out from the cracks in the walls, and shaggy grass with brown stalks covers the roof. In the entrance that faces the sea there is a motorcycle workshop—the floor stained with black oil, rock music blaring out as though it is a nightclub. The building has a stone plaque which names it Villa Generale

Vincenzo Traniello, above which is the only mention of King Ferdinand II that I could find in Gaeta. The fabric sign has an arrow pointing to 'Re Ferdinando II Ristorante Pizzeria'. Of course the pizzeria, like much of the rest of the town, is now closed.

The Italy that Conaci and Dirimera saw was fragile, and in just ten years it would be gone. The local kingdoms and elite societies would be broken down and would merge into something larger, the fiction of nationhood that was sweeping Europe. Now many people outside Italy will tell you this fiction has become fact—that Italy is indeed a nation. But despite one hundred and fifty years of living with the idea of nationhood, those inside Italy identify not with the country but with the city or the region. Italian society turns inwards not outwards, and always has. Italians wrap themselves in their region, their town, their street and finally their family, in ever-tighter bandages of dependency, love and loyalty. Only those who, like Conaci and Dirimera, arrive in Italy unprotected by these layers, and live close enough to see them, can understand how little the nature of its people changes over time.

⌣

Conaci and Dirimera set out with Salvado to their new school—at Badia di Cava de' Tirreni. Their journey followed the sea south of Naples, turning inland when the landscape became mountainous, passing the steep slopes of the Amalfi coast. The horses puffed and ploughed through forest—bright green and cool even in that hot, muggy summer. Their hooves trampled dry, crunchy leaves and passed thick burrs and thorny vines of berries.

Eventually, after a few days of travel, the boys saw it in the distance—the Baroque facade of Badia di Cava de' Terreni's church, high on the mountainside. Seemingly small, this facade hid the mass of monastery buildings behind it, stretching along one side of the valley. Behind this, the forest reached up and stopped at the higher levels of the mountains, to reveal the peaks: grey, rocky stubs stretching towards the sky.

For Salvado this landscape was familiar—this was where he had completed his training to become a monk with Serra and where they had decided to become missionaries. Salvado's monastery in Spain, at Santiago de Compostela, had been ordered closed when he was just twenty-one years old, and he had made his way from Santiago de Compostela back to his parents' home in Tuy. He helped his father administer the Salvado estate, gave music classes to local women and children, and played the organ in the cathedral.

This ordinary daily life was refreshing and dangerous for the newly ordained monk. He soon became afraid of falling in love with a young woman who shared his love of music. Not much is known of the romance, but the Tuy Diocesan Archives contain some music scores composed by Salvado at this time, entitled 'Fantasy, Variations and Ending', 'Grand Fantastic Waltz' and 'Small Entertainment with a Marching Tune', all for pianoforte. They were not religious or dance songs but romantic pieces both captivating and difficult to play, according to music historians. Their dedications read: 'To the virtuous Miss Paquita Patrelli', 'To Countess Lobioliourna' and 'To Marquess Santasila'.[5] Since it is likely that the countess and marquess were patrons or perhaps students of Salvado's, it may be Miss Paquita Patrelli who captured his attention. But Salvado's guilt and sense of religious devotion weighed upon him, and he talked the bishop into overlooking his age and bringing forward his priestly ordination.

Salvado had kept in contact with Serra, who wrote from Naples that he had gained a position as lecturer in theology at the nearby monastery of Badia di Cava de' Terreni. Most of the monasteries outside Spain, and particularly those in Italy, were overcrowded with monks from other countries who had been driven out by revolutionaries and liberals. The secularisation of United States missions in 1834 closed another outlet for homeless monks. So, Salvado's chances of continuing his studies and becoming a monk seemed impossible, and he asked for Serra's help. By September 1838 Salvado had been at home for three years and was believed to have been contemplating marriage, when a letter arrived from Serra saying that he had at last been granted permission to invite Salvado to continue his studies with him at Cava.

On 9 September, Salvado left Tuy for the main Galician port of Vigo, where he took a ship for Naples.[6] Within five months of his arrival, on 23 February 1840, Salvado was ordained to priesthood in a nearby church in Nocera dei Pagani, and a week later he celebrated his first Mass in the chapel at Badia di Cava de' Terreni. It was his thirtieth birthday and an auspicious date, as Salvado was to write in his memoirs: 'The first of March is for me a memorable day for four reasons: it's my birthday, it's my feast day, it's my first Mass day and it's New Norcia's foundation day'.[7]

High in the rocky mountains outside Rome, the Badia di Cava de' Tirreni was isolated from other towns, and life there continued in much the same way for Salvado as at Santiago de Compostela. But due to its isolation and distance from family, there were fewer distractions from religious study and prayer. Another key difference was that at Cava the older Serra became a teacher of theology for Salvado.

From all accounts—positive and negative—Serra was a person who made an impression on those around him and seemed to have no doubt in his own convictions, despite external challenges to their truth. Abbot of Silos and historian Luciano Serrano described Serra as 'of a rather rough nature, rectilinear in his ideas and convictions'. He was also intelligent and, since he was a child, Serra had excelled at Latin. At Cava, Serra taught Theology, Canonical Law, Greek and Hebrew. During this time, Serra and Salvado's convictions became noticeably stronger. As Linage Conde describes it, 'We have the impression that the trauma they experienced due to the death of their monastery and congregation and being exiled from their country, had also been a purifying experience individually for them'.[8]

Not long after he was ordained, Salvado was appointed as a warden, music teacher and organist. He ordered a new organ, which was finished and enlarged by the monks over three years—it had 84 registers, which was 34 more than the renowned organ in the monastery of Monte Cassino. Concerts were held, attended by the King and Queen of Naples and the composer Saverio Mercandente, who became a lifelong friend of Salvado.[9]

Despite the uprisings against the Church across Europe, a papal and monastic revival took place during Salvado's time at Badia di Cava de' Tirreni. Rome followed the instructions of Pope Gregory XVI's encyclical *Probe Nostis*, published in 1840, which set the goal for the nineteenth century to become 'the mission century'.[10] Salvado and Serra talked about this goal during their regular walk in the woods outside the monastery, and on the morning of 11 July 1844, Serra blurted out, 'There is something really magnificent about these missions and I feel deeply attracted to them—there is nothing finer a man may do—but on the other hand …'.

Salvado, who thought he was pausing at the prospect of the risks and hardships of being a missionary, 'broke in and asked him if he would be prepared to go if I went with him':

'If you can face it, I can too,' he replied, 'as long as we go together.' This was all I needed to hear, and with a heart full of joy, I told him of my plans and a few preliminary steps I had taken. We went on talking for a long time, and then agreed to seek further light in prayer about this momentous decision. There was no sleep for us that night, with our minds ceaselessly revolving about the foreign missions, and the points for and against them. The following evening when we compared notes about our state of mind we found that far from weakening in our proposal, we were even keener and more determined than before; as a result we decided to consecrate ourselves unconditionally to the missions among the native peoples.[11]

Serra and Salvado left the monastery at Cava on 26 December, and on 29 December they went to the Vatican to talk to Monsignor Brunelli, Secretary of the Sacred Congregation for the Propaganda of the Faith. He told them they were needed in Australia and put them in touch with the Irish Father Brady.

Over a month later, Serra and Salvado's application was approved by the Sacred Congregation. On 14 February 1845 Brunelli told the two monks they were to go to the Sydney mission. They penned a letter to their Superior at Cava asking permission, and then went off to visit the Monastery Del Sacro Speco at Subiaco. This holy site— said to be the cave where Saint Benedict retreated from the 'degenerates' in Rome—held much significance for Salvado, who noted in his diary:

> In that cave, the cradle of the order of Saint Benedict, the saint who restored European civilisation we the humblest of his sons said Mass and entrusted our cause to our great leader and father, asking that our work should redound to the good of the Faith to which he had dedicated his life.[12]

Salvado describes how he felt shaky on leaving the cave to return to the light of day.[13]

Before they were to leave Italy, the party destined for Perth sought an audience with the Pope. On 5 June 1845 Brady, Serra and Salvado visited the Vatican to see Pope Gregory XVI. An 86-year-old Camaldolese monk, Pope Gregory had weathered the anti-religious winds crossing Europe. He sought hope in the foreign missions for spreading the faith, and told the assembled party destined for Australia:

> Remember that you are sons of Saint Benedict, our great founder. Remember all those Apostles who were your brothers, who converted whole peoples and nations to the faith and educated them in the ways of civilised life. Remember that you are setting out on the same road as was trodden by them. Do no dishonor to the monastic cowl which you wear. Go then and Heaven will bless your holy desires.[14]

He gave Bishop Brady a small crucifix and Salvado and Serra each a silver medal with his craggy portrait on one side and an image of the Lord sending out the Apostles on the other. Three days later Salvado left Italy behind, headed for Australia.

Now Salvado looked fondly at the expanse of the monastery where it had all begun, Badia di Cava de' Tirreni, remembering the comfort of the forest paths where he had walked so many times, the familiar sound of the river rushing through the valley. He recalled his decision to go to Australia with Serra and to leave his fellow monks for a less ordered, more adventurous life.

To Conaci and Dirimera the monastery represented an adventure outside the realms of their experience that was about to begin. It was the first time they had seen Badia di Cava de' Tirreni and it seemed an unnatural place— the mountains so high, the forest so dense and green, the buildings so preposterous on that isolated slope looking towards a settlement in the far distance, near the sea.

The horses followed the river and Conaci and Dirimera bumped together in the carriage as it lumbered over uneven stones in the road. Reaching the base of the monastery, they crossed a bridge to the other side of the river and climbed up the paved cobblestones to make the final winding S-bend of road to the monastery's door.

Salvado jumped down from the carriage and rapped on the door. It opened to reveal the abbot who once had Salvado under his care. When Salvado and Serra applied to become missionaries while they visited Rome, their Superior, Abbot Candida, refused the monks permission to leave Cava. It was a move motivated by his appreciation for the two, particularly Salvado, as Candida later revealed in a letter to Salvado:

> We thought it was a great blessing to have you as our companion and it was equally a great loss to one and all when you left. How valuable your presence would be to the monastery today, especially to the many youths about us whose hearts may be affected by the teachings of an atheistic world and whose minds need instruction in the principles of piety and learning. Your name is still closely associated with our organ and when at its best during ceremonies it never fails to remind me of you.[15]

However, the Church bureaucracy urged the two monks to stay in Rome while they sought the abbot's permission, and their powers of persuasion did not fail. The two monks received another letter from Abbot Candida, saying he had reflected on their perseverance and gave them permission and blessing to go abroad. Now, five years later, he welcomed Salvado with open arms and cooed over the young black Benedictines nervously hiding behind Salvado's robes.

As they entered the monastery the boys walked across its coat of arms, which depicted, in inlaid marble on the floor, a black schoolboy's hat, a cross, a crown and twelve tassels, symbolising the twelve monasteries Saint Benedict had established in Italy. Conaci and Dirimera had entered one of the oldest monasteries in Europe. Founded in 1011 by Saint Alferius and enlarged by his successor, Abbot Peter, the monastery began in an underground cave. Over the years the monks carved the walls of the grotto into arches, smoothed them and painted the stone with depictions of the prophets. Conaci and Dirimera saw on the stone walls of the cave the smiling Mary, with almond eyes and blond hair and dressed in a red robe, flanked by Saint Benedict looking worried and carrying a long staff, and another monk, his face blurred but holding open a Bible.

Also in the walls of the cave they saw a carved pledge of allegiance to the Pope in Rome, a legacy from the time in the 1300s and 1400s when two Popes, one in France and one in Rome, had warred for supremacy over the Church and its estates. Monks had hidden in these underground chapels in times of troubles from the first century onwards. In these dark, aged caves Conaci may have lingered over the black bird painted in the centre of the ceiling, Spirito Santo (the spirit of God). Age had made it just a shadow of the bird it must have been when freshly painted, but it still recalled his namesake, the black cockatoo, its wings outstretched in flight.

Above the caves, the boys walked through the Norman arches of white marble and granite forming an underground courtyard with a fountain in its middle. The natural rock overhung half of the space, letting in a little light but hiding the monastery's centre from the outside world. Roman tombs, covered in griffins, dogs, wild boars and soldiers, also rested in this cavernous space.

They made their way upward from this holy cave and into the school. The Baroque expanse of the monastery was all light white borders, and pastel stencilling, and paintings of Saint Benedict, and cherub-like children with blond hair and wondrous faces. It was a labyrinth of corridors and rooms, and the two boys kept close to Salvado, knowing he was soon to leave them behind.

The boys were set up in a room together, furnished sparsely, with the king's generosity providing two desks and two beds, and a window looked out into the forest on the slope opposite. They set their trunks down, for what was likely to be a long time. In them were clothes others would no longer see—for now each day would be spent in the black robes of novices.

Although Conaci was at this stage about nine years old and Dirimera about eleven, the boys were put in a class with much younger children, so they could be introduced to the languages of Latin and Italian along with the youngest novices.

Once the boys began studies, Salvado went away for a few days to make preparations for his journey home to Australia. To his disappointment, the Papal Secretary told Salvado, in Naples, that the Pope had decided to make him Bishop of Port Victoria (Darwin) and, in spite of his protests, he was consecrated in this role on 15 August

1849. He then returned to Cava to check on how Conaci and Dirimera were faring. This short meeting is described in his diary:

> I asked them if they were happy and well, and they told me that they were better off than at the Mission, which I am sure was true.
>
> 'I am leaving tomorrow,' I told them. 'Do you want to come back with me?'
>
> 'No!'
>
> 'And why not?'
>
> 'Because we have not done our studies. When we go back to Australia our parents and friends will ask us if we understand the talking papers [letters] and if we can make them ourselves [write], if we can make horses and trees and many other things [draw] and if we tell them that we can't do these things they will tell us that we are still junar or bush people as they are. So it is much better for you to leave now; in the meantime we will study a lot, and when we can understand all the talking papers, can sing, and play with the fingers [musical instruments] and say Mass, which we like very much, we will make you a talking paper and you will come to meet us at the water [Fremantle] with two horses. Then we will leave the walking house [ship] and us two boys will go off into the bush in different directions and we'll bring all the boys we find to the Mission school. Just now we don't know anything, and

we'll teach school to others; but soon we'll be able to—you'll see!'

This line of reasoning, surely above what one could expect of their age and condition, filled me with joy. How much good will these two boys be able to do for their compatriots whose blood and language they share, whose beliefs and way of life they understand? May God bless them for His greater glory, and for the good of the souls of the poor unfortunate natives![16]

∽

Badia di Cava de' Tirreni is an inspiring place—as I walked along its ornate walls, stared out at the mountains all around and the sky, bright and seemingly close at this height over the sea, I thought of Salvado and Serra's visions with some nostalgia. As I climbed the steps to the monastery library, I thought of Salvado's depiction of his conversation with Conaci and Dirimera, elements of which are undoubtedly correct, but which tells only a portion of the truth.

Were the two boys, so shaped by Salvado and the notion of 'the grand experiment', saying what Salvado most desired to believe? He himself had said of the Yuet people, 'Their shrewdness is such that they always shape their replies to what the questioner wants to hear—and they are able to read faces so well that they are aware of even hidden thoughts'.[17] Or was Salvado not listening but hearing what he wanted to believe—transferring his ideals on to real children, wiping out their fears and doubts, and perhaps even his own, with a superimposed certainty, strength and simplicity?

Salvado's record of this conversation with Conaci and Dirimera strikes me as written by a man in love. Salvado was infatuated with a grand experiment, the purpose of which was not to test a theory but rather to prove an ideal: to verify his personal ideal of God, man, civilisation and religion, and to justify all that he had sacrificed in its pursuit.

The Archives is a room where the walls are stacked high with wooden drawers, each labelled by century in neat Roman numerals on a brass plate, and each containing documents from those hundred years. The librarian at first did a quick tour—a wedding certificate from the third century, a Bible from the fifth— but when asked, assured me that there were no records of the 'Benedictine Australianos' in the meticulously kept archive that spills over into three rooms. The grand experiment is not recorded in the history of this grandiose archive, and I felt Salvado's disappointment at its absence from the annals of the monastery he loved so much.

⌒

Salvado left the boys in Badia di Cava de' Terreni and travelled to Spain, where he returned to his home town of Tuy in Galicia. On 4 September 1852 he was received with great pomp at the Tuy Cathedral, the place where he had been baptised thirty-eight years before. His baptismal entry at the Tuy Cathedral reads:

On the 2nd day of March, 1814, I, Don Juan Francisco Pineiro, Parish Priest of the Holy Cathedral of Tuy, solemnly baptized there a child who was born the previous day, to whom I gave the name Lucas Josef Rosendo, legitimate child of Don Pedro Salvado and Maria Francesca Rotea. Paternal grandparents were Domingo Salvado and Tecla Perez who, with the father of the child, came from San Miguel de Tabagon, feoff of San Bartholomew of the Threshing-floors. The maternal grandparents were Francisco Antonio Rotea and Anna Maria Nuñez, deceased; the latter a householder of Tuy, but native of San Justus and Pastor of Entienza. The former, together with the mother of the baptized child, dwell in, and come from Tuy. I instructed his God-parents Don Lucas Portela and Dona Josefa Figueiroa, both householders of Tuy, about their obligations to the baptized and I hereby certify it with my signature as Priest.[18]

These people had now gathered in the cathedral, along with his abbots and fellow monks, to see the man known to all as Rosendo Salvado, his common name indicating Saint Rudesindus and his father's name. On this visit Salvado saw his mother for the last time. He left behind an environmental legacy by introducing the eucalypt into Galicia and nearby Asturias. In the town of El Pito the first tree raised from Salvado's seeds was a local curiosity, and an avenue of eucalyptus outside the cemetery of Los Muros was established.[19]

⌒

In the forests of Cava, Conaci and Dirimera were adjusting to a childhood to be spent in preparation for the monk-hood. They were to be schooled in the Benedictine tradition, which had a particular idea about what made up a monk.

The word 'monk' comes from the Greek '*monos*', which means alone. The first person to earn the title '*monachos*' (the one who is alone) is believed to have been Antony, an Egyptian who lived in the second and third centuries. He gave up his possessions, sent his sister into a community of virgins, and retreated from the world into the Egyptian desert. The Benedictine tradition was to take a different concept of the monk—one pioneered by Pachomius, who lived in large communities of like-minded people called '*koinobia*' (from the Greek '*koinos*', meaning common).

Saint Benedict, born in 480 in a small town called Nursia, north of Rome, was to take this idea of the *koinobia* and popularise it, establishing twelve monasteries around Rome and writing a set of rules for such com-munities. These rules made the search for God the primary focus of a monk, who was supported in a community of peers undertaking the same quest. Such is the weight given to peer pressure from the community that individual will is discouraged in all affairs.

After his death in 542, Benedict's Rule was adopted across much of Europe through patronage of Pope Gregory

I. So popular was the Rule that the French ruler Charlemagne asked his advisers 'if any other rule was in use, and others could wonder if there had been monks at all in Europe before Benedict'.[20]

The first word Saint Benedict writes in his Rule is 'Listen'. The Rule places great emphasis on the importance of silence in which to find God. On its first page it states: 'Let us listen with attentive ears to the Divine Voice warning us, daily crying out ... "Come my children, listen to me, I will teach you to be God-fearing folk." Run while you have the light of life, lest the darkness of death overtake you.'

So one of the key principles of Conaci and Dirimera's education was to learn to be still and silent:

Life and death are in the power of the tongue ... it is right for the master to speak and teach, and proper for the disciple to be silent and listen. So if anything has to be asked of a Superior, let it be done with all humility and respectful submission. But as for buffoonery, or useless words, such as move to laughter, we condemn them to perpetual exclusion from all parts of the monastery and forbid the disciple to open his mouth in such discourse.[21]

Monks were forbidden from talking except at set hours, and corporal punishment was used for boys who were caught breaking silence. Conaci and Dirimera must have hoped that their Superiors paid heed to the Rule's advice that 'due proportion should be observed in the treatment of all, according to their age and understanding', and not 'whenever boys and adolescents ... commit faults let them be punished by severe fasting or painful stripes, that they may be cured'.[22]

The boys learnt Italian, Latin, the Bible and the Rule. They would have learnt of the twelve stages of humility to which all Benedictines must strive: 1) fearing God at all times, 2) not loving one's own will because 'self-will has its punishment, but necessity wins a crown', 3) accepting obedience, 4) enduring with patience through trials, 5) 'not hiding from one's Abbot any of the evil thoughts that seek entrance to the heart or sins committed in secret but humbly confessing them', 6) being 'content with the cheapest and worst of everything', 7) 'in addition to a verbal reckoning of himself as lower and of less account than all he also makes it part of the inmost belief and feeling of his heart', 8) 'doing nothing that is not authorized by the common rule of the monastery or the example of the monk's Superiors', 9) 'refraining from speech and remaining taciturn and silent until questioned', 10) 'not being easily and quickly moved to laughter' and 11) speaking 'humbly and seriously, briefly and sensibly, and not noisily'.[23] The final step, the twelfth, is humility:

[a monk] not only has humility in his heart but also gives continual evidence of it by his very deportment to all who see him: at the Divine Office, and when he prays in the

oratory, and where ever he may be in the monastery, in the garden, on a journey, in the fields, whether he is sitting, walking or standing he has his head always bent and his eyes fixed on the ground always mindful of the guilt of his sins and imagining himself already present before the dread judgement seat of God.[24]

The Rule is exhausting to read, let alone live by in its literal sense, and the only saving grace for Conaci and Dirimera may have been if their Superiors had the usual Italian flexibility around set times and rules. The abbot kept their personal possessions under his watch unless they obtained special approval. The boys probably slept in their monks robes, as the Rule instructs, so that at all times boys appeared decorous, even on waking. It is also likely that the boys were kept occupied from dawn till dusk, as the Rule instructs that every hour must be spent studying or working on minor tasks such as cleaning, because 'idleness is an enemy to the soul'.[25]

They seem to have developed basic Italian language skills within about six months of arriving at the monastery. Salvado believed that this was due to the similarity between the rolling musical qualities of the Italian and Yuet languages

[The Yuet language is] not at all harsh or guttural as is usually the case with Oriental languages nor does it have the unpleasant whistling that is observed in most Oceania dialects. On the contrary, it is endowed with deep and sonorous sounds very similar to the harmonious ones of our language and as flexible and soft as the best Italian ones. It is sufficiently rich to express the few needs of its speakers so that they in a few words expressed like maxims communicate their ideas with as much energy and sweetness as we do with the abundant riches of our language.[26]

The linguistic talents of the two Yuet boys meant they were able to keep up with Mass and other ceremonies, many of which Salvado had already taught them on the mission and during their journey together. In the monastery's chapel, encased in white marble interspersed with beige, red, grey and black marble and borders of gold roses and leaves, the softer voice of Conaci and the deeper one of Dirimera blended with the other boys in song. They looked up to a monk at the altar, which was supported by columns of twisted marble inlaid with geometric golden tiles, in turn held up by Roman lions carved from marble, the lions' mouths open in a grimace, their legs strong and muscular.

At least three times a day and often five, the boys would pray together in silence. The only respite from the quiet was when they were allowed to walk through the woods—or at night, after the monks had left, when small voices spoke with a sound so practised that it could have been mistaken for the rustling of leaves in the valley.

Still boys, not teenagers, Conaci and Dirimera must have snatched moments of play, a few daydreams, the occasional squabble between themselves in their times alone. They must have thought of home, of the flat, dry land so different from all these slopes and trees, of the absence of women so marked compared to the role of their mothers, grandmothers and the circle of elders who tended to them in their camp. At times they must have longed for the freedom of tribal life, where they could run, laugh, play and talk with the women all day. Their bodies were lithe and restless while their minds strained to understand their new world, new language and new religion.

Both made progress, but Conaci was more adept at learning and it must have been difficult for Dirimera to be compared to one so bright. When the boys had learned enough language to write a letter in Italian, ten months after their arrival at Cava, it was written jointly—but was probably penned by Conaci while Dirimera talked at him. Salvado was so proud of the letter that he included it in his official diaries:

Very dear Rosendo,

We very glad get your letter, and we very glad you well. We plenty pray God for natives and you. Why you not come monastery new moon? You come quick quick we like very much. Us very well and happy. Me, Francis, study well; John, John, Father Master, whole three. You pray for

Francis and John at Mass. We want picture too. Father Master kiss your hands and all my friends. Kiss your letter, kiss your hand, you give blessing.

> Cava 24th June 1850
> Francis Conaci
> John Dirimera[27]

This is the boys' letter in its original Italian:

> Carissimo Rudesindo,
>
> Molto noi piace ricevuta lettera tua, e molto noi piace state bene. Noi molto pregare Dio per Australiani e voi. Perchè tu niente venuto monastero luna nuova? Tu venir subito subito a noi fare grande piacere. Noi stare bene assai e contenti. Io Francesco studiare bene; Giovanni così così, ma sempre portare meglio. Tu baciare piede Papa, per Francesco e Giovanni Padre Maestro tutti tre. Tu pregare per Franscesco e Giovanni a Messa. Noi volere una figura pure. P. Maestro baciare mani te, e tutti miei compagni.
>
> Noi baciata lettera tua, baciata mano te e dona benedizione.
>
> Cava 24 giugo 1850.
> Francesco Cònaci
> Giovanni Dirimera[28]

Another letter a year later showed that both the boys had made progress from pidgin Italian to a degree of fluency. Still, the divide between Conaci and Dirimera in their schooling and their outlook is obvious between and on these lines. Conaci's letter reads:

Your Lordship,

It is with great pleasure that we received your welcome letter, dated 1st July, by means of which we learnt that you are in good health, and we assure you that we are too. We hope that your occupations will leave you free at least for a few days, so that we can have the consolation of seeing you again and kissing your hand.

To give you a proof of my behavior in study, I send you a certificate that I got in the public examinations of September, with the mark 'Very Good' together with the silver medal which the Father Master of Novices is keeping for me.

John has profited little or not at all in his studies and has not learnt to read. In one thing he has made a little progress, and that is writing as you see here enclosed.

We thank you for the picture cards of saints that you have sent us, and we ask you bring us a little book of prayers containing the Preparation for Holy Communion. We kiss your hands affectionately, as do all my comrades, especially Brother Silvano. Asking your holy blessing,

I am

Your affectionate son in Christ

Francis Xavier Conaci

Cava 18th July 1851.[29]

In the original Italian it reads:

Illustrissimo Monsignore,

Con sommo piacere ricevemmo la vostra carisima con la data I luglio per mezzo della quale conoscemmo che stavate bene in salute, lo stesso vi assicuriamo di noi. Speriamo che le vostre faccende vi lasciassero libero almeno pochi giorni, affinchè potessimo avere la consolazione di rivedervi e baciarvi la mano.

Per darvi un attestato della mia condotta nello studio vi rimetto un decreto, che ebbi nei saggi pubblici di settembre insieme alla medaglia di argento col grado di 'molto bene', la quale tiene conservata il P. Maestro.

Giovanni poco o niente ha profattivo neglistudie fina no ha uncora imparata leggere. In una sola cosa ha fatte qualiche poco di profittocia nella calligrafia come sechete qui appresso.

Vi ringraziamo delle figurine di santi che ci avete mandate, e vi preghiamo a portarci un libretto di orazioni dove vi sia il preparamento per la SS. Communione. Vi baciamo caramente le mani e fenno lo stesso i miei compagni specialmente D. Silvano; e chiedendovi la santa benedizione mi soscrivo.

Vostro Aff.mo figlio in Cristo
Francesco Saverio Cònaci
Cara 18 Luglio 1851[30]

Their teacher, Father Gaetani, added a note in the margins, 'The above letter, composed and written by the boy himself, shows how proud he is and how little attention he pays'.[31] If Conaci had become proud, raising his head high, Dirimera had his lowered in resignation. His letter reads:

> Most Illustrious and Reverend Monsignor,
>
> Your letter pleased me beyond expression and from it I realised that you, thank heaven, enjoy excellent health, and it also shows me that you still remember me.
>
> I will do my level best to stick to my studies and to carry out your wishes, however poor and neglected I may be. I will not cease praying for you to God that he grant you all the graces that your heart desires. I ask heaven's blessings for you and I kiss your ring.
>
> Your son in Jesus Christ,
> John Dirimera[32]

This is as Dirimera wrote it:

> Ultimo e Primo Monsignore,
>
> La sua lettera mie giunta gratissima oltre orni dire, tra perche nerileso che Ella grazia al cielo gode florida la salute, tra perche mi da'a conoscore che serba tuttora memoria di me. Io mi studiero a tutto uomo attendere agli studi per adempiere ai desideri di lei quantunque porerissimo e negletto mi asessi ligegno. Non mai poi

lascero di alzare preci Altissimo per lei, accio la colmasse
di tutti quelle grazie che il suo cuore sa desiderare. Le chie
do la S.B e col bacio del Sacro Anello mi segno.

Il suo Siglio in Christo,
Giovanni Dirimera.[33]

Later that year, around Christmas in 1851, Salvado
was to see Conaci and Dirimera for the last time. As the
horses drew his carriage up the mountain road towards
the monastery of Cava, Salvado saw a group of novices
walking down the slope. He noticed that two were dark-
skinned and ordered the coachman to stop the horses. He
jumped down and waved to them.

When Conaci and Dirimera recognised him, they ran
towards Salvado and kissed his hands in the traditional
greeting. Together, they walked up the road talking, and
Salvado gave them a few religious mementos. The next
morning, when Salvado attended Mass in the marble
chapel, Conaci climbed the steps to the altar, held up by
ancient Roman lions, and read a Latin lesson. Salvado
was delighted to see that 'the language was familiar to
him'.[34]

Salvado stayed at the monastery for over a week, each
day talking to the boys and spending time with them.
They must have asked questions about home, but Salvado
only had news second-hand from Serra and is unlikely to
have known much about how Conaci's family, in particular,
was faring. Salvado must have noticed that Dirimera,

having less success in communicating in Latin and Italian, was participating less in monastic life, but if he detected any melancholy in the boys he ignored it.

As he parted from the boys, to return to Australia, he called them 'my children'. Conaci and Dirimera watched his carriage wind down to the valley and then down the riverside path. Looking out the window at the lush greenery and the boys, smaller and smaller behind him, Salvado felt assured that the grand experiment had been a great success.

Outside the monastery I walked down the old road, cobbled with dark grey stones, stepped and winding to make it easier on the horses' hooves. Walking over the rushing river, I wondered whether it had always been so covered with blackberries, vines, large lilies and other green undergrowth that ran riot through the valley. Under the trees the temperature drops significantly and the forest encompasses people with a blanket of quiet—punctuated solely by the rushing of water, swaying of branches and chirping of crickets. Lizards scattered away as I walked, imagining the dark robes of monks brushing against the nettles and weeds that lined the path.

I thought of Salvado and Serra walking these tracks and deciding to become missionaries. Despite their education they would scarcely have known how different the Australian bush would be from these green, steep, dramatic slopes, always cool, even in summer. I thought of how their experience of plunging into a totally different environment was not so dissimilar from the transition that Conaci and Dirimera made in coming from the Australian bush to this mountainous valley. Still, Salvado and Serra were adults who had made a choice, a commitment in their minds and hearts to change, to travel, to leave the comfort of monastic routine and familiarity behind them. Conaci and Dirimera had little choice, or one that they could have not understood at such a young age and with so little experience of the world outside their tribe.

I thought of Conaci and Dirimera here on these forest paths: two black faces in the gaggle of white children, leaning towards each other to whisper a few words of their own language under these trees.

The isolation, loss of familiarity, necessity to acquire a new language and customs were experienced by the boys and Salvado alike, as they travelled from one side of the world to the other. They had to lose all that they knew, and this made them wide-eyed, naive and inherently vulnerable. By crossing the globe they put themselves at the mercy of their new surroundings, and all became fate's children.

After a few years at Badia di Cava de' Terreni the star pupil, Conaci, began to feel unwell. He sweated more and felt hot, sometimes dizzy and at other times nauseous. It was not dissimilar to the illness Dirimera had had when he first arrived at Cava and into which he now relapsed as well, causing them both alarm.

The Abbot of Cava warned Rome in early March 1853 about the serious condition of the Aboriginal novices. He took them to doctors, including the Pope's physician, who diagnosed chest complaints aggravated by the climate. The abbot asked the Congregation for the Propaganda of the Faith for funds, so that they could be sent back to Australia. He wrote that although they were only fifteen and twelve years old, he deemed them sufficiently civilised to be missionaries. Between the lines may have been his concern that whatever Conaci had seriously and Dirimera mildly was contagious and would spread through the school and its teachers.[35] But funds were not forthcoming, and so the abbot decided that in the meantime they should be sent to Rome, while the authorities organised a passage home. The boys' few possessions were packed and they were bundled into a carriage bound for the monastery of St Paul's Outside the Walls.

Coming Home

*A*fter the quiet of Badia di Cava de' Tirreni, Rome was more loud and rambunctious than the weakened Conaci could bear. A ship sailed them up the River Fura to the monastery of San Paulo Fura le Mura (St Paul's Outside the Walls) monastery. Standing alone on a plain above the river, it was a tall and square, with the austerity of a fortress. Only one side of the complex suggested the ornateness within—it opened on to a colonnaded courtyard and was peaked by a mural-covered second storey depicting the Lamb of God with a gold halo around its holy head.

The small ship docked at the jetty that had been built for the Pope's visits to San Paulo. Conaci and Dirimera were met by a monk, who led them up the hill and ushered them into the cool rooms of the monastery. He gave them beds and a few days to recover. Shortly after this rest, Conaci's condition improved a little and he and Dirimera joined the others in study.

Conaci and Dirimera had arrived in one of the oldest and most revered monasteries of Rome. The first Benedictine community is testified to by a piece of marble that records the monks and nuns who lived there at the time of Saint Gregory (509–604). In the Middle Ages the monastery was walled and the coat of arms created. It featured the Abbot of St Paul, represented by an inscription around a sword and a belt of leather, and the threatening motto: *Honi soit qui mal y pense* (Shame to him who thinks evil of it). A bone of Saint Benedict was preserved in the Capella delle Religuie, and the monastery and cathedral of St Paul's were rebuilt and consecrated by Pope Pius IX in 1854. Just finished when Conaci and Dirimera arrived, the building's marble must have shone as if it had been taken from a full moon, and the grey stone of the walls was clean and new. The site smelt of dug earth and shavings of wood. St Paul's had risen from the ashes of fire thirty years before to be one of Rome's great churches, considered second only to that of St Peter, near the Vatican. The school, too, was one of Rome's premier monastic institutions.

However, Conaci and Dirimera were often lethargic and spent many hours lying in their rooms sweating and having difficulty breathing, and no doubt talking in snatched whispers about their new surroundings. Far from the eucalypts of home, through the windows they could see tall cypresses, pines and oaks in the countryside that surrounded the monastery.

Sometimes at night they could hear the rush of the river, which must have reminding them of the Cava they had left behind, the sea that had taken them so far from home, and even the bubbling stream that ran through their own land when it rained. The stronger Dirimera would have helped Conaci to church for Mass, where the space itself must have been yet another reminder of the boys' frailty

⌇

From the outside the basilica seemed large and plain, but when I stepped inside the detail of each layer from ground to ceiling made it seem even more immense—and it is; the scale is staggering. As I walked in from Via Ostiense, a small offshoot of a room features a marble statue of Saint Benedict, with a long wavy beard and long staff curled at the end. Then the centrepiece on the ceiling— Jesus and four disciples in mosaics littered with gold drew the eye upward.

All around, the amount and variety of marble is thrillingly dense and cold—yellow marble cut thinly becomes heavy windows; red, green, black and grey marble is cut into rectangular blocks and lines the walls. The floor is entirely grey and white marble, and the white marble statues of saints are white. A huge medieval candlestick carved from marble stands near the church's centre, its spiralling pictures of battle and triumph more crude and old than its nineteenth-century surrounds. Two rows of marble columns line the church, topped by a ring of carved leaves, but their bases are swat and plain. Round painted portraits of the Popes hang high on the walls, their backgrounds gold, and the latest Pope is illuminated by a golden spotlight. Pius IX sits as sombre as the other Popes, with his large eyes unnoticed by most visitors.

After visiting this impressive space I had an hour or so to wait before the cloister, a popular place for snapshots, was open to visitors. On the west side of the monastery is an open V-shaped park with long lanes of gravel lined by trees. I sat on the grass, leaning against the pine, and wrote of having a soft, creeping feeling of purpose and peace. I had an unexplainable certainty that the question I had come to Rome to answer—'Where was Conaci?'—would be answered. It was anticipation without nervousness, a sense that the pieces of information Conaci had left behind were about to fall into place.

In the cloister of San Paulo Fura le Mura I waited until the tourists from Portugal had left and I had the courtyard to myself. Arches held up by spiralling coloured-tile columns framed the courtyard, where roses grew and a large round marble bath sat in the middle, with a fountain of trickling water. It felt familiar, and I thought of the time my mother and I had visited a similar courtyard in Italy and she had seen an old woman, dressed in black, sweeping a corridor with a stick broom. When we looked her way again she was gone, and we speculated that she might have been a ghost. As I was thinking this, a pigeon landed on the side *of the bath and had a drink. As I tried to take its photograph it flew away, up into the blue sky.*

The next morning, I arrived as scheduled at San Paulo Fura le Mura at nine. To my carefully rehearsed 'Bonjourno. Ho apuntamento con Padre Evandro', the aged doorman replied 'You are the Australian!' We laughed and he picked up the phone to dial Evandro, but the phone rang out. He expressed puzzlement, explaining that he had seen Evandro that morning, and tried again. The phone rang unanswered. The doorman got up from his desk, walked to the bottom of a large marble staircase and shouted: 'Padre Ev-an-dro!' At the top of the stairs appeared a thin, tall man—bald with black sideburns and round black glasses— probably in his thirties. 'Si!' There followed much discussion about the phone, questions about whether it was working and affirmation by both sides that indeed it was not. Finally, Evandro picked up his phone and dragged it on to the stairs to show it to the doorman, and they discovered, amid laughter, that the cord has become unplugged.

I was then introduced to the smiling Evandro, who took me inside the archives. A high-ceiling room, its wall-to-floor shelves are accessible by wooden ladders. Evandro pulled out three boxes from a bottom shelf. In one box was Salvado's handwritten diary, in Italian, from the 1800s. At the back of this journal was his carefully transcribed dictionary of Yuet words, in columns titled 'Nord' 'Sud' and 'Italiano'. It seemed surreal to handle such a document.

Padre Evandro was writing a thesis on the reorganisation of the library and, while he discussed this and the rebuilding of St

*Paul's Basilica after the fire of 1823, he had difficulty
understanding some of my questions. An English-speaking abbot
was called, and the monks discussed my questions regarding the
grave of Conaci and the records of his death. Eventually we found
the journal entries of the historian Gregorio Palmieri for 1853,
the year the boys were brought to St Paul's.*

⌒

On the first page of his journal, Palmieri set himself up
as a storyteller, beginning with the florid prose: 'As the
year burst forth, amidst many trials and great turmoils…'
Turning to the month of Conaci's death, October, a
section entitled 'The Story of the Australian Benedictines'
recounts the arrival of 'two young savages' in San Paulo
Fura le Mura:

> The first boy was Francis Conaci and the second Giovanni
> Dirimera. He [Salvado] presented them to Pope Pius IX
> in Gaeta who condescended with his own august hands to
> clothe them in the Benedictine habit. Therefore the two
> Australians were two new alumni and were put in the
> alumnate of the monastery of the Holy Trinity of Cava.
> They began to learn languages—Italian and Latin—and
> Conaci especially demonstrated a good and precise capable
> memory … The air of Cava did not present itself to the
> two Australians in favourable ways … Monsignor Salvado
> pleaded to translocate them from Cava to Saint Paul's

Outside the Walls where effectively they arrived if I am not mistaken in the middle of June 1853. Ugliness of their forms, their skin colour truly black and the red of their eyes and eyelids rendered them brutally ugly. But treated gently they turned out docile and collaborative and in the church devout. One of them, the better Francis, was however sick—and not a little. It seems that in our climate their blood heated up and their chest did not resist atmospheric variations. Nothing was said to us about the sickness of the poor Conaci but the facts became obvious. The evening of the 17 September, being Saturday, the Master of the School, in the chapel of the alumnate, was hearing confessions of the youngsters when in haste he was urged to come quickly because Conaci was in the act of purging his stomach and had lost all feeling. The Master of the School ran immediately to find him still trembling and was just there in time to give him and to administer the extreme unction [last anointing] because he then passed away immediately from this life.[1]

Conaci's funeral was celebrated the next Monday at the grandiose Church of St Paul's. His coffin would have looked so small in that huge space. Perhaps they heaped it with flowers, perhaps they left it bare as befitting a novice's striving for simplicity. The high voices of Conaci's young fellow-students and the low voices of the monks who were his masters would have sung his last hymns. After the service, the coffin was carried outside and slowly lowered into a plot in the communal burial ground of the monks at the foot of the '*campino*', meaning countryside.

⌒

Where is the campino? I asked. The monks told me it was now a stretch of grass, partially paved, on the west wing of the basilica. The place where I had sat yesterday, describing in my journal a feeling of peace, was precisely where Conaci's bones lay.

Later, in Western Australia, I read in a new light the following account of Salvado's first killing of a wild animal:

> *By chance I found myself in the midst of a flock of cockatoos and I hurled my stick at some who were close together. I was lucky enough to kill one with a blow to the head and break the wing of another. I picked them both up, but the wounded one kept up such a terrible screeching that all the others began to wheel round my head with loud cries as if trying to rescue it. Although I do not think I am a particularly timid man, I was afraid for my life, for if this cloud of five or six thousand furious birds had attacked me with beak and claw it would have been all over for me. Meanwhile, I hastily knocked the wounded bird on the head and dodged behind one tree after another, and thus saved myself from reprisals.[2]*

As I finished reading these words, I thought of how Conaci, named after the black cockatoo, also lost his life due to Salvado's unwitting actions. I looked up from the journal and noticed a drawing that had been there all the time, but that now made the hairs on the back of my neck stand on end.

Just before I visited New Norcia for the first time and saw the photograph of Conaci and Dirimera that sent me to Italy to find out what had happened to Conaci, I made a pencil sketch of a black cockatoo. By intent or accident, it was a depiction of the young boy his parents called Conaci: a young bird, the black feathers on its head unfurled and excited, the red on its face flushed, its eyes sparkling with expectation and its beak ready to release the squawk of a creature about to take flight. He perched just long enough in the tree of life for me to notice him, before he flew away, into a dreaming that only he and his ancestors can know.

Thinking of this, I walked out of the archives into the summer sun, and to the west wall of the basilica again. A young boy, dressed in shorts, ran towards and away from, then towards and away again from his mother, on the white stones of the pavement. Despite the traffic and shops, peaks of the hills around St Paul's, rocky and steep, can still be seen. I could see Conaci's burial ground as it would have been when he was placed there, as countryside—a flat piece of land in front of a rocky hill that dips into a slope leading to the copper-blue currents of the Fura River. I thought of how much of Rome must be built over forgotten bones, just as the white basilica of St Paul's now shadow's Conaci's dark, unmarked grave. It was with a heavy feeling that I realised I could see the burial place that Conaci's parents and siblings could not have imagined, let alone visited.

⌐

Records indicate that Conaci's father, the person who had named him after the black cockatoo, died in the same year as his son, from a common Western disease. What Conaci died of remains unclear—it could have been cholera, bronchitis, glandular fever, or simply a common cold or chest infection of the kind that struck down so many Aboriginal people at the time.

Conaci's silver medal for being outstanding in his class at Cava sits in the museum in New Norcia as a reminder of what he achieved, but there are few mementos of what he lost. Was his family told of their son's death? Or did his father, Malanga, die before he knew what had happened to his beloved son? Was his family still out in the bush, unreachable by the monks? If they were told, did they express anger or betrayal, or did they simply listen and go away to mourn amongst themselves? There are no records, in Salvado's diaries or elsewhere, to describe what happened and what Conaci's family thought or felt or knew.

⌐

Dirimera was once again alone. He had begun this journey a sick boy in the company of monks. Conaci's presence had given him some companionship and reminders of home, but now there was nothing. He withdrew into his own thoughts and refused to talk or associate with his fellow pupils, behaviour which only furthered his isolation. Palmieri, in his account of Dirimera's stay, tries to explain his depression as a cultural trait: 'Dirimera was slower of learning. He did not entirely cast off the proud character of the savage.' In his view, the problem with Dirimera was that he was taken away from his tribe when he was too old and 'he was already inside the customs of his tribe and had been a cannibal'. According to Palmieri's account, Dirimera was feared by the other pupils due to his seemingly inhuman behaviour: 'Dirimera did not show any reaction to the death of his companion, in fact, it was necessary later to take him from the alumnate and consign him to the particular direction of Padre Camille Le Duc of the Abbey of Solesmes who however was not able to reach him or take him away from his savage habits or customs'.

Dirimera's patrons had abandoned him—the King of the Two Sicilies was preoccupied in a final fight to preserve his reign; Salvado was now a diocesan administrator of Perth, and Church politics had taken him away from the affairs of New Norcia.

Letters were exchanged between monasteries about what to do with Dirimera. One written in October 1853 from the Benedictine College in Douai, France, advises that he be forwarded to London immediately, but adds this caution:

It appears to me we should be running some risk if the youth were to take this long journey and voyage during the winter months. The ships to Swan River [Perth] are very few in number, compared to those who go to other parts of Australia. The youth might have to wait in London five or six weeks.[3]

Fortunately, the other founder of New Norcia, José Serra, was in Europe and heard of Dirimera's condition. Dirimera himself wrote to Serra on 29 September 1851:

> Dear Monsignor Serra,
>
> I hope to study enough and return soon to Australia, kiss the hand of Papa Nalbinga like others and Mama Callango and embrace my brother Ciari and again like sisters Uggiana, Nalbuna, Jauna, Uibungo and greet all of my people. I kiss your hand.
>
> Your affectionate son in Christ,
> John Maria Dirimera.[4]

> Carissimo Monsignore Serra,
>
> Io sto bene e contento spero di studiare assai e ritornare presto nell'Australia. Bacio la mano al Papa, cioe Gnalbinga come altersi alla Mama Calcianco, ed abbraccio il fratello Ciari, come ancoraste sorelle Uggiana, Nalbuna, Jauna, Uibungo e saluto tutti I miei Compacsani.
>
> Vi bacia la mano.
> Il V° Affmo. Figlio in G.C.
> Giovanni Maria Dirimera.[5]

Records of Dirimera's trip back home are scarce but it is believed he met with Serra in London, where together with four French nuns they boarded the *Lady Amherst* bound for Perth on 31 January 1855.[6] Reaching Perth two months later, on 22 May, Dirimera's condition had worsened but, remarkably, the rough conditions at sea had not killed him. He saw doctors in Perth, but they could not help the boy with an undiagnosable chest condition and a scar wound in his stomach. Dirimera had difficulty breathing, felt weak almost constantly and would lose consciousness when the pain became intense.

〜

A Nyungar artist who speaks the Badimaya-Yamatji language, Julie Dowling, has taken stories of her great-grandparents and depicted them in a style that combines Western realism and a traditional Aboriginal style and subjects. One of her paintings tells the story of her great great-grandmother, Melbin, who was taken to Cardiff in Wales as an 'exhibit' when she was nineteen and returned pregnant with Julie's great grandmother. But it is her comment made in relation to one of her many self-portraits that echoes the life of Dirimera so long ago: 'My family believes that when a person is sick that their spirit is taken back into the land and that only your family can make you well again'.

〜

Dirimera might have had a sense of this when he finally reached New Norcia mission. There were his parents, clothed, married, workers now on the mission, but reassuringly familiar—still his family.

He refused to live on the mission and went off with his parents and brother into the bush. There are reports that his family lived together in a hut and tended to the sick boy.[7] By this stage, Dirimera had been ill on and off for five years. He had survived the travel across the world to Badia di Cava de' Terreni, from there to San Paulo Fura le Mura in Rome where he lost Conaci, from there to London where he finally secured a passage home.

The Yuet word '*cala*' means fire but also has the same meaning as 'home and hearth'. It is the word the tribe used to express that feeling of being physically and spiritually at home. Dirimera now experienced *cala* once more, but the joy was sharp and short.

Dirimera died, surrounded by his family, on 21 August 1855, when he was about seventeen years old. They took his body back to the New Norcia mission for a Christian burial. Salvado was still in Perth and could not attend the ceremony. The day after Dirimera's death he wrote in his diary: 'The Australian, John Dirimera died after receiving all the sacraments and he was buried after the vigil and sung mass behind the church of New Norcia. He was the first Aboriginal Australian to be buried on the mission as a Christian.' His grave, like Conaci's, is unmarked today and no plan remains of the graveyard to signal where he lies.

Unfortunately, like many members of his tribe, some of Dirimera's family would soon follow him to the grave. His younger brother, Miguel, died one year later, in September, from a common but undiagnosed disease. Then a letter dated 25 December 1857 to Salvado, from Father Garrido on the New Norcia mission, reported: 'Yesterday, Christmas Eve, was saddened by the funeral of Callango, mother of Juan María Dirimera and Miguel, both now dead. It was difficult to restrain the widower, Nalbinga, from seeking an innocent victim.'

It was the tribal custom that when someone revered dies, a person should be killed. Clearly, the grieving Nalbinga, having lost both his sons but not 'the proud character of the savage', as Dirimera had been described, wanted the traditional recourse for the loss of his wife. Father Garrido reassured Salvado:

> [Nalbinga] was eventually calmed down, and was pleased with the Christian burial which Callango had requested, as were the many other natives who attended the ceremony. She was interred in a coffin, near her two sons, after lying in the church overnight which also pleased the natives.[8]

Nalbinga's final expression of grief befits his son's personality, which was always more distant and fierce than his more sociable companion, Conaci. Dirimera remained a 'proud character' until the end, a survivor with much to tell but few means to tell it. We can only wonder what he told his family of his time abroad, of the people he met and those monks in which his parents had placed such trust. We can only imagine the loss Dirimera's family felt when he returned to them not triumphant but exhausted by all that he had experienced and the little he had gained. We can only guess at what his true feelings were about the pact his family had signed him to, and whether he resented it. Still, it is easy to imagine their joy and tears on his return—how the family would have bonded again and sought solace in their land.

The unmarked graves of Conaci, Dirimera and their families stand in contrast to the many monuments lauding the life of Salvado, who by dint of his charismatic personality is remembered as the primary founder of the New Norcia mission. Late in his life Salvado once more left Australia for Europe, where he hoped to confirm the monastic status of New Norcia by uniting it to the monastery of Montserrat—set high on mountainous fingers of rock in Catalunya, Spain. In a letter to the Abbot of Montserrat, Salvado wrote:

> Some have asked me whether I was frightened to undertake such a long and painful journey at my advanced age of 85 years and 7 months. I answered that I was not in the least frightened; that I was enjoying good health, thanks be to God, and that I felt I was fulfilling a sacred duty, whatever be the outcome of it.[9]

Salvado received a royal welcome at Montserrat, the authorities of which attributed to him a part in founding the missionary college in 1885. From Montserrat he gathered together a celebrated music teacher and three priests to come back with him to New Norcia and join the mission. However, his plans to accompany them to Australia were thrown awry when he became ill in Rome and, like Conaci, was lodged at the monastery of San Paulo Fura le Mura.

Death came from exhaustion rather than a definable illness. On 29 December 1900 Salvado received the last sacraments of the Church and then passed away, reportedly muttering the names of Aboriginal children from the mission and moving his hands and fingers as though recalling them to himself.[10] The plain room in which he died at St Paul's is still called the Salvado Room.

Salvado's body was taken back to New Norcia. His large stone tomb bears a portrait of his face carved into the dark rock and these words, in Latin: 'Here in the Peace of Christ / Awaiting the Glorious Resurrection / Sleeps / Rosendo Salvado O.S.B. / Titular Bishop of Adriana, Founder / and First Abbot of New Norcia'.

There is one monument to the grand experiment itself in the town of Tuy, in Spain, where Salvado was born. Tuy has been carved out more by nature than by human design. It rests on a slope that tilts upwards to northern mountains of native oaks. These trees, rising straight from slanting soil, cover the characteristic green peaks and curves of the province which Tuy guards: Galicia.

The stone buildings of the town sit square and stare at the Portuguese town of Valença on the other side of the valley. At the bottom of the terraced streets and lanes, flanked by granite walls, is the River Minho—a natural border with Portugal, drawn sometimes in murky green and on other days by grey, rushing water. The river is both the link with the outside world and a defence against it, a playground of beaches and pools, but with a perilous current pushing dark-soiled water from high mountains into the cold blue of the Atlantic Ocean.

Tuy's history has been dictated by a key Galician trait: stubbornness. In the Galician mind, this is not a flaw but a virtue. Without it, Tuy's land and religious tradition would have been lost in its infancy.

The tribe that settled on this slope was known as Tuivi and, as they built more dwellings, the place itself became known as Tuy. As it became a small city, the Romans took control, but the town was better suited to the Visigoths, who made Tuy the centre of their kingdom after King Witiza invaded and established his court there in 698. After a little more than a hundred years of peace, in the eighth century, the Visigothic realm was besieged by the Moors, who took over large swathes of Spanish land, changing its architecture and land in ways that hold strong today, especially in the south. But Tuy remained defiant and independent under the protection of Don Pelayo, a man whose legend ranks with that of Britain's King Arthur. He was the first Christian King of Galicia—idolised at the time and studied as one of the key historical figures of the region for centuries afterwards. His town, Tuy, became a Spanish symbol of resistance against the Moors and Islam.

By the twelfth century, peace had been restored and Tuy's status as a Christian settlement entrenched. A primitive Gothic cathedral was built overlooking the stone houses as a reminder of the virtues of defiance and as a call to fishermen working in the river below—it was dedicated to their patron saint, San Telmo.

Periodic fights with the Portuguese ceased after the Middle Ages and Galicians near the border picked up the Portuguese style of lyric songs and certain traits of their language. Foreign goods and ideas from the colonies overseas soon reached Tuy thanks to fishermen and traders, but still the town remained culturally Galician.

Galicians particularly clung to their church, rejecting anti-religious trends and holding tight to tradition and folklore. One such legend stated that the corpse of Saint James had sailed up the Ria de Arousa and so had come to rest in Galicia. A hermit was led by a bright star to the place where Saint James's corpse lay one night. That site became known as St James of the Field of the Star— Santiago de Compostela—and from the twelfth century onwards pilgrims came to this place, wearing the scallop shell, for the feast of Saint James on 25 July.

Saint James's shrine at Santiago de Compostela captured the imagination of Christians and became their third most holy site after Jerusalem and Rome. It is not surprising that by the eighteenth century, churchgoers in Tuy thought their religion was not an import but a natural part of the land and the people that had defended belief so vigorously.

Today, a visitor to Tuy can walk along a street known as Calle del Obispo Salvado. Here, an elegant three-storey home with balconies and windows overlooking the terraced gardens and fields leading down to the River Minho has a plaque near its door which states:

On 1st March 1814 there was born in this house the Bishop of Pt Victoria and latterly of Adriana, the Apostle of New Norcia, Western Australia, the most illustrious and Rt. Rev Rosendo Salvado. (The sons of Tuy dedicated this tablet to his glorious memory. Tuy 7/4/1902.)

The statue of Salvado and two Aboriginal boys is found close by. The words on the monument of course are all about Salvado and read:

Born of noble parentage at TUY in Spain, he chose the life of an Apostle. Overcoming difficulties almost innumerable, with infinite labour he planted Faith and Religion in the hearts of the Aborigines. Adorned with a heroic soul, simplicity of manner, and every virtue he was a model preacher of the GOSPEL.

Having shed lustre on the Catholic Church and on his Religious Order, he died as he lived, in the odour of Sanctity, at the monastery of Saint Paul, outside the walls of Rome, on 29 December 1900, in the 87th year of his age, the 70th of his monastic profession and the 51st of his Episcopacy.

The monument itself to Salvado and his boys is a sculpture of a missionary with his hand raised in blessing and at his feet two young Aboriginal children, their figures carved to resemble Africans more than the Indigenous Nyungar people of Western Australia that they represent. The missionary stands on a column, holding his face to the sky. At the base of Salvado's column an Aboriginal boy sits around a slack-postured infant as they both stare at something in the elder boy's palm.

The sculpture manages to have a touch of realism and surrealism at the same time—the facial expressions of the three figures are almost cartoonish while their forms reveal, in three dimensions, the fall of their clothes and the tautness of muscles. It is a small stone representation of the story of a Spanish monk and two Nyungar boys who together had pursued an unprecedented quest known as 'the grand experiment'.

Findings of
the Grand Experiment

If my piece opens the concert it could be titled 'Contemporary Overture' and if not then 'A Miscellaneous Fantasy'.

Rosendo Salvado, letter dated 23 June 1873[1]

Salvado, Conaci and Dirimera shared a love of music. It was a common trait of the Yuet people—a natural musical ear, a heart moved by sound. In Salvado's diaries and the boys' letters, Conaci and Dirimera's musical sense comes across—their wonder at hearing regimental music, their unprompted affirmation of their enjoyment of Mass, their imitation of new sounds, their wonder at new languages. As for Salvado, even at an early age his primary-school teacher commented that he had a 'sharp mind' and an 'affection for letters and the arts, with a special predilection for music', and he later taught and composed music.[2]

One piece of music that remains is both a Yuet and Spanish creation: it is Salvado's musical notation of a Yuet dancing song that can be played on the piano. As a piece of music, it is simple, lifted with an engaging pace that leaves no time for reflection. As a dance for the tribe, it would have been lively and animated. Salvado named the song *'Maquialó'* (Dance) and, together with the Yuet tribe, he would sing it:

> Not once, but hundreds of times, when they were stretched out on the ground, weary and sick of the work, if they heard me sing Maquialó which is one of their most common and favourite dancing songs, they got up, as if seized by some irresistible force, and not only sang the refrain, but took to dancing in fine fettle—the more so because I joined in with them … The advantage of this for me was that, after a few minutes of this, I would call out cheerfully 'Mingo, mingo' which literally means 'breast' but is used where we would say 'Come on!' and they would gradually start working again and this time with so much energy and zest that it seemed that the Maquialó dance had put new life into them.[3]

The dancing song would have been used at corroborees. These were rare times when various Nyungar families and tribes came together in a spirit of peace to hunt, make fires and music. Three or four hundred people would gather on a level stretch of ground plucked free of stones and grass. A large fire and a number of small ones were lit and kangaroos were hunted and eaten. Men then decorated their heads with feathers and dog tails and painted their bodies in white and ochre. A respected elder, the corroboree master, started the dance. He headed a single line of people, and as he moved the others imitated him. Music was made by keeping time with the feet, and at every second step they uttered heavily accentuated sounds in unison. After one song they did the same for the second most respected person, and so it went on into the night. Some songs imitated the story of a hunt, and dancers mimicked animals and men. The music told a story passed down from generation to generation and from tribe to tribe.

On an old piano in the heart of Sydney, the traffic creating a wind outside the window, I tried to play the 'Maquialó', and after a few practices I got into the fast pace and light notes undercut by the bass that plods in time, suggesting a drum or heavy rhythm stick. As the notes rang out from the keys, I felt it as a celebration of life, but one with the calamitous peak, the knowledge that this festivity is soon to end. As a song of a people, it is a brief gasp of joy at the potential of a tribe, their place and their spirit.

Dirimera was the only child of 'the grand experiment' who returned alive. After his death in the bush, three more children were taken to Europe, but all died of

Western diseases shortly after their arrival overseas, and the mission gave up hope of educating pupils abroad.

The few girls taken from around New Norcia and placed by the monks with the Sisters of Mercy in Perth also met with early deaths. The first Yuet girl to be given a Western education had accompanied Salvado to Perth and narrowly escaped drowning when their wagon was overturned by a current of flood water. She was baptised Maria Christina and kept her Nyungar surname, Cucina.[4] Sister Ursula later reported of the twelve Aboriginal girls who came to the Mercy Convent School, 'They received the Sacraments regularly and with great devotion but civilisation seemed to be more than they could bear. They all died young.'[5]

For those who stayed on at New Norcia itself, many of Dirimera and Conaci's tribe died when measles spread among the Yuet people in 1860—just as their own families had died of Western diseases.

When Salvado arrived in the 1840s, about 250 Yuet people lived around the pool on the Moore River winding through the Victoria Plains. This was before agricultural settlement had its full impact on the local population. There were more adults than children (who were 40 per cent of the population) and more men than women (who made up only 40 per cent of Yuets).

It is believed that few, if any, descendants of the tribe with which Salvado was in contact have survived. Today their language is found in small entries in old documents.

Nyungar people in the area today are believed to be descended from many tribes and from both white and black parents.[6]

The findings of 'the grand experiment' were discussed by the colonial and Church elite of the time, both of which were split between positive and negative views of the Nyungar people. Some, such as Daisy Bates, a researcher for the Western Australian government in the early 1900s, interpreted the case of Conaci and Dirimera as proof that Aboriginal people could neither live in European society or benefit from higher education:

> In Australia, the gradual disappearance of the natives, who, before the advent of the white man, had existed for ages upon the land, continues without ceasing, notwithstanding the many and constant efforts of the respective Governments towards reclaiming, civilising them and arresting their downward course ... Various religious bodies have vied with each other in their attempts to rescue the Aborigines from oblivion, but with doubtful success.[7]

Discussion in Italy about 'the grand experiment' was similarly dour. The archivist of San Paulo Fura le Mura, Gregorio Palmieri, commented in conclusion about the stay of Conaci and Dirimera in Rome that 'the experience showed that the education of the Indigenous people is difficult and only possible at the mission itself'.[8]

When the Perth-based newspaper, the *Inquirer*, reported on 2 January 1850 that Conaci and Dirimera had met with the King of the Two Sicilies and been admitted into the school of Badia di Cava de' Terreni, the editor could not help but add a note of disdain, 'Should these Neapolitan Noblemen ever return to the colony, we have not the slightest doubt that they will quickly sink in their dignity and again resume their bush habits'.

In the Western Australian government, views towards the local Nyungar people were similarly fearful and dismissive. Dr R. R. Madden, Salvado's friend and godfather to Conaci and Dirimera, lambasted the governmental assembly in 1849 for their indifference to concerns raised at their meetings over the 'ill-treated native population', and he soon returned to Ireland.

While attitudes of many authorities in Perth may have been regressive, they were not shared by all. In his memoirs, Salvado was keen to point out alternate views of settlers towards the local tribes. He cited Sir James Stirling's comment that 'many among the natives are highly intelligent and with very acute perceptions', and that of local farmer George Moore:

> The natives are not so despicable as a race as was at first supposed. They are active, bold and shrewd: they are quick of apprehension, and capable of reflecting on the difference between our manners and customs of their own, in a degree you would hardly expect.[9]

Many people made mention of the usefulness of Nyungar people in the bush. Yuet people could find their way around during the dark, and their knowledge of direction was derived from the feel under their feet and the smell of the bush as well as their sight. The Yuet, like most Aboriginal people, made excellent trackers for white settlers, amazing all who employed them in this capacity.

In Britain as well as among well-meaning settlers in Australia, there was concern about the colonial treatment of the Aboriginal people and the bleak outlook for their future. A presentation to the Meetings for Sufferings in London in 1842, just four years before Salvado and Serra set out for Australia to establish a mission, stated: 'That the Aborigines have been losers instead of gainers by the settlement of the whites amongst them is beyond dispute; they have contracted if not all the vices of the Europeans at least many of them and none of their virtues'.

While the rights to land of Indigenous people were ignored, it is overly simplistic to say that the British merely abused and ignored Aboriginal people. At forums such as this Meetings for Sufferings there was a great deal of talk among educated elite about the undesirable situation in Australia and how their settlement had failed to offer the Aboriginal people any hope of economic or social advancement. With evidence presented from clergy and settlers of Australia, the meeting reported:

It is denied that there is any such mental incapacity as to prevent them [Aboriginal people] from becoming, in time, intelligent and useful members of the community. This is apparent to every one who has had the opportunity of observing the shrewdness and natural quickness of observation they possess in a high degree. Where the experiment has been tried to educate any of them it has perfectly succeeded. All are not apt alike but this cannot be expected— there is a widespread prejudice afloat on this subject at home and abroad.[10]

Humanitarians in Britain publicised the issue, and alarm spread for the wellbeing of indigenous people throughout the empire. These concerned parties came to wield enough political influence to affect government policy if not their deeds. In 1836 a parliamentary select committee investigated the situation of Aboriginal people in Australia, and its report went to the British parliament. The following year the British government stated that its objectives were to secure for Aboriginal people due observance of justice and protection of their rights, to promote civilisation among them and to lead them to peaceful and voluntary reception of Christianity.[11] Of course the linking of the welfare of Aboriginal people with Christianity was to lead to many more interventions into their lives and further missionary zeal in the British colonies.

While now, in hindsight, the paternalism and folly in 'the grand experiment' become clear, in the context of the times Salvado's thinking was progressive. When he admitted Conaci and Dirimera to the school at Badia di Cava de' Terreni, it was fifteen years before the United States abolished slavery, France and many other nations had not yet secured modern democracy, Europe was ruled by kings, the world was dominated by empires, and the notion of individual rights and respect for other cultures was in its infancy. Much of Salvado's energy was spent trying to prove the humanity of the Nyungar people to British and European people, so they would not be treated as mere animals:

> The physical and moral character of the Australian Aborigine has been falsely represented for many think of him as the most degraded member of the human race. He is thought to be puny, deformed, and not very different from the brute beasts, some going even so far as to say that he is indistinguishable from the orangutan. Quite a number of people deny that that poor native has a rational soul.[12]

A great portion of his diaries is spent advancing arguments to the contrary—about the beauty, intellect and morals of the Yuet people.

It was hoped that 'the grand experiment' would at least dispel the idea that the Nyungar people were intellectually inferior to white settlers. Salvado had speculated that 'As far as their intellectual powers are concerned, there is every reason for thinking that if these are carefully trained, they will succeed in every form of education both in the arts and the sciences'.[13]

Salvado accentuates the familiar aspects of the appearance of the Yuet people, just as by washing and cutting the hair of Dirimera and Conaci he tried to style them as being like Europeans. He kept a lock of each boys' hair in his diaries. It is unclear whether the note underneath the hair is Salvado's, as it is written in English while the other pages are written in Spanish, but it says, 'Hair of the natives—red and long—drew great admiration from all, especially from African natives'. By having hair that was a different colour and texture from that of Africans, Salvado hoped that Nyungar people would be seen in a better light by Europeans:

> Some boys of six or seven years of age, in particular, had limbs of such distinction and beauty that they surpassed the finest creations of Greek sculpture ... The women, especially those of marriageable age are also quite well built ... Indeed if in addition to the beauty of their limbs, and the liveliness of their black eyes, they had long and well-arranged hair, they would differ from European women only in the colour of their skin.[14]

Of the women, he consistently mentions their caring and moral nature in an effort to counter the idea, wide-spread in Perth, that Aboriginal women were 'loose'—many having been raped by white men or taken as wives, and a few being prostitutes. Salvado writes that within the tribe, relations between men and women were proper: 'In the three years of my stay in the interior, I have never seen any unchaste or indecent behaviour among them; on the contrary I have found their behaviour very creditable indeed.'[15]

As the tribe began to decline rapidly in numbers due to disease, the monks drew up a marriage-tree to indicate who could marry who. Salvado knew the genealogies of the local families and their social organisation, and attempted to preserve the tribe as a social grouping.

Much of the debate around 'the grand experiment' focused not on the individual achievements of Conaci and Dirimera but on this question of whether extinction of indigenous peoples was inevitable. When Charles Darwin's book, *Origins of Species*, was published in 1859, in the same decade as Conaci and Dirimera's deaths, many seized on his theory of 'natural selection' to argue that indigenous people were destined to extinction as a race in Australia, Africa and elsewhere.

Daisy Bates wrote in her report to the government entitled *Efforts Made by Western Australia towards the Betterment of Her Aborigines* that despite education and other interventions into the lives of Aboriginal people, little progress had been made to improve their situation. About Salvado she concluded:

Not withstanding the devoted labours of Bishop Salvado amongst the Mowera (local Yuet people) natives, in spite of his life-long efforts towards the amelioration of their condition and his strong desire to bring civilising influences gradually into their lives, the results have proved his inability to cope with unknown forces. That mysterious law of nature which seems to doom all savage races to disappear on the advent of the white man amongst them continues to exercise its inscrutable functions and through that law the ultimate disappearance of the Aborigines is apparently but a matter of time.[16]

Many Aboriginal tribes all over Australia had already been reported as being extinct. Edward John Eyre, the noted explorer and Lieutenant-Governor of New Zealand, reported in the late 1850s that 'In Sydney, the Port Jackson tribe, which in 1788 numbered 1500 had in 1839 become extinct; in Tasmania the last Aborigine died in 1857'.[17] Bates reported at the turn of the century:

In Perth the last female Swan River native died on March 20th 1907. In Guildford but one old native remains of the once numerous Guildford people, and all along the Western Australian coast line where the closest settlement has been, the Aboriginal population is slowly but steadily vanishing.[18]

Florence Nightingale, who corresponded by letter with Salvado to complete her research, laid down in *Note on the Aboriginal Races in Australia*, published in 1864, what she thought were the causes of decline in Aboriginal populations: the introduction of liquor, use of Indigenous women as prostitutes, hunger resulting from deprivation of hunting grounds, attempts to civilise Indigenous people by interfering with customs, poor sanitary conditions as a result of being confined in schools and other institutions, plus cruelty and ill treatment.

In later life, Salvado came to recognise the cultural and spiritual effects of taking Nyungar people from their land and families. We can only speculate if he knew or considered Dirimera and Conaci's experiences as part of this cultural loss. Dirimera, particularly, showed obvious signs of depression towards the end of his life, due to abandonment in Europe, the loss of Conaci and his time apart from his family.

There is one mention in Salvado's correspondence of his own doubts and feelings of loss when he first came to Australia and established the mission when: 'If I tried to relate in detail my life during those three first years, whoever tried to read it would be covered in darkness'.[19]

In his later years Salvado wrote about the 'nostalgia' of Nyungar people and how it affected their will to live:

For some time he goes on well, gay and full of life, but in a few months, or perhaps after a couple of years a fatal melancholy takes possession of him. Being asked what is the matter with him he answers, 'Nothing!'

'Do you feel sick?'

'No Sir.'

'Do you suffer any pain?'

'No Sir'

'Why are you not so cheerful as before?'

'I do not know.'

He takes his meals as regular as ever, he has no fever, but he daily and almost at sight loses his flesh, strength and health.[20]

Daisy Bates wrote that 'Salvado consulted many of the chief medical men of Europe over this and other similar cases and almost every one of them came to the conclusion that nostalgia or "home sickness" was the name of the malady'.[21] Clearly, few people had an understanding of the cultural and emotional effects of white settlement and the resulting breakdown of traditional Aboriginal life.

When Salvado returned to the New Norcia mission, his ambitions were more modest than the education and introduction into Western Australia of black Benedictines. Just as in his letter about his musical compositions, his 'grand experiment' had now become a 'miscellaneous fantasy'. He turned to more practical pursuits, planting 400 olive trees in 1866, around 250 of which survive today. His plans for the local Nyungar people had been reformed by experience, as is illustrated in his writing about famous Aboriginal people who had been taken to the West:

When Governor Phillip, who founded the colony of New South Wales, came to Europe in 1792, he brought with him the native whom he called Bennelong. On his return to Australia in 1795, Bennelong threw away his European clothes and rejoined his own people in the bush and when he was found there by the Protestant Chaplain Mr. Marsden he assured him that he was very happy to have re-found his freedom. Another native whom the English call Daniel, from Parramatta, was taken to London by the naturalist Cowley and he too on his return to Australia went off into the bush to merge with his own people. It is supposed to be a great kindness to have taken Bennelong and Daniel to London and to have introduced them to illustrious families. But what was the point of it? Was it to make them in any way better off? No not at all! They were taken around to be shown as rare objects, or perhaps even as two animals dressed up as men. Were they, for example, admitted to any school or college? How many acres of land were they given when they returned home? How many oxen, cows, sheep or other animals? What about the agricultural implements, the seed for grain and the other things needed for working a farm? Without any of this, Bennelong and Daniel were worse off than their fellow-natives because they now had greater needs and less means of satisfying them. And what of their moral education? Not long after Daniel went back to the bush, he raped a young white woman and was sentenced to death. This was the result of what he saw of life among the white people.[22]

Clearly he did not see Conaci and Dirimera's experience in the same light as that of Bennelong and Daniel. Rather than stressing higher education, or even Christianity, Salvado saw that the Yuet people in his care at the mission would only survive if they found an economic role in the colony. Paid employment, he considered, rarely offered satisfactory reward for effort:

> Often a native's work is equal to the white man's but a settler would think it quite ridiculous to pay him anything, especially ready cash. The result is that everything is to the advantage of the white man and the native who gets only such a pittance as charity demands leaves the settler and returns to the bush where reunited with his family he not merely enjoys the freedom that was his birthright but can usually fare better in general than in his employer's household.[23]

Florence Nightingale, too, came to advocate what she called—ironically, considering the failure of 'the grand experiment'—the 'Salvado method' of treating indigenous people, which was to be pragmatic and practical. She criticised the Protestant and Catholic missions alike and concluded: 'The wiser Missionary of this day says: "What is the use of reading and writing to the native?" It does not give him a living. Show him his duty to God and teach him to plough.'[24]

Salvado himself, in his 1864 report to the Western Australian Legislative Council, stated: 'I think that in civilizing the Aborigines of Australia the learning of the A.B.C. etc ought to be a secondary thing; religious instruction and physical work, both at the same time, ought to take first and leading place'.

He recognised the skill of Nyungar people with animals and directed them to the breaking and mustering of the endurance horses that the mission bred to sell to the British Army in India. The explorer John Forrest, after using one of New Norcia's horses to ride to Adelaide, sold the horse for ten guineas, which was reportedly the second highest price paid for a horse in the country in the late 1800s.

Monks at New Norcia also taught the local men how to shear sheep, at which they proved to be especially skilled. Salvado reported that in 1867 an Aboriginal man had sheared 990 sheep in 25 days, and a youth 838 sheep.

For all Salvado's goodwill, few Yuet people who came into contact with him ended up better off in terms of their status and rights within the settler community. Certainly, through his focus on finding paid work for Yuet people, Salvado did not advance those interests of Aboriginal communities that would be fought over in modern times—such as land, and freedom to live under tribal rules and to govern their own affairs.

Towards the end of his life, Conaci and Dirimera were a distant memory—and one of the first helpers at the mission, a man called Bilyagoro, was also in dire straits. Salvado had written from Rome in 1867 to intercede when Bilyagoro was sent to Rottnest for a minor offence, most probably stealing or drunkenness:

> I know well that man since 1846 and in all truth I do not know any other native of Western Australia of a more quiet and peaceful character than he is or at least he was. In settling quarrels among the natives he has been, on many occasions, a great help to me, and I positively know him to be, or to have been, a peacemaker even when alone with other Aborigines. Moreover, I ought to add that he has a right to my gratitude for his great services to me in my first years in the bush—services that no money can pay.[25]

The stories of Conaci, Dirimera, Bilyagoro and many other Nyungar people were part of a broader story of the subjugation, whether through good intent, indifference, hate or neglect, of Aboriginal people across Australia. Salvado's lofty ideals for the Yuet people, like his 'grand experiment', failed in practice. However, the monks' presence did provide a space where Nyungar people could live with their families. Without this, there would have been no buffer between the Yuet people and some of the worst impacts of white settlement, such as alcoholism, sexual abuse, unpaid labour and imprisonment. And the education that Salvado and the other monks provided did help some people get jobs on neighbouring properties and so provide for themselves and their families.

Perhaps the most surprising part of the story of 'the grand experiment' was how little of this trial was observed, noted, discovered and learnt from. The effects of contact with Europeans on the health of Aboriginal people was made only after whole tribes had been wiped out by introduced diseases. Even then, these deaths were not seen as a problem requiring action but tended to be depicted as a sad but inevitable part of progress. The psychological and cultural damage done to generations of Nyungar people through the loss of their land and interference in their tribal and family affairs was slowly recognised, but it did not prompt greater respect or sensitivity to their culture. Instead, many began to fear that all that had been done to Aboriginal people was bound to result in reprisals. This was the view of Archbishop John Polding, who wrote to Salvado:

> The advance of civilisation, its march, is the march of extinction. If other measures, which our liberal governments reject, are not adopted, the native black will soon disappear. And blood calls for blood. It is a question of time. But this proverb will be fulfilled.[26]

Salvado himself saw the work of the mission as a success, as he makes clear when writing to the Society of the Propaganda of the Faith for the last time in 1893:

It is forty-seven years since I arrived in this part of Australia, to devote myself to the conversion of the unfortunate Aborigines who were considered as being no better than wild animals. Thank God, this is not the case today, since, in view of the incredible results obtained in this holy mission, the question of the ability or inability of the Australian aborigines has been resolved and decided in their favour.[27]

There was a certain stubbornness in Salvado's pursuit of the civilising of local Nyungar people even after doubts had been raised by many over the benefits of this process. Although in the 1840s there were several church-run schools in Western Australia, by 1847 all but New Norcia were closed, because of financial constraints or the fact that parents had reclaimed their children to protect them from the diseases running rife in the classrooms.[28] Salvado had once written to Bishop Christopher Reynolds of Adelaide:

Nothing can conquer patience and perseverance, if led by prudence. Those three Ps, if conjoined, constitute a power which I think can never be subdued—and no work of any importance could be done if those three Ps are wanting and much less if none of them exist.[29]

Salvado sacrificed prudence in his perseverance with the Yuet people. Even after the measles epidemic had killed many of the families he had come to know when he first arrived in the bush, he *continued* to recruit Aboriginal children from beyond the Victoria Plains area, and he was influential in changing the local Education Act in 1871 to require Aboriginal as well as white children to attend school.[30]

After Salvado's death, the mission and its education of local Nyungar people continued. It took in Indigenous children as boarders—often young boys and girls who had parents, despite calling itself an orphanage. In the late 1800s parents and children began to publicly resent the breaking up of their families in the name of Government and Church education goals. When the monks began to restrict access of parents to children, matters reached a crisis point. Thirty-five Aborigines, led by Emmanuel Jackamurra, George Shaw and Lucas Moody, stormed the New Norcia mission orphanage in 1907 to free their children. Their efforts were unsuccessful and the three men were arrested, charged and convicted—they were locked in prison for two months for 'disorderly conduct' and another month for the damage done to mission property.[31]

The orphanage closed in 1973, and now New Norcia stands more as a monastery than as a mission. In the movement towards reconciliation in the late 1990s, many faiths apologised for the damage caused by their role in taking children from their families over the centuries since Australia's settlement. The psychological and social impacts for both children and parents has now been widely acknowledged. In Western Australia alone, the Aboriginal Legal Service collected six hundred testimonies of people who had been taken from their families by Church or Government authorities in recent decades. Unfortunately, Conaci and Dirimera's experiences were only the beginning of a long history of intervention in Aboriginal family life by those who thought they knew better.

Governor-General William Deane in 1996 put forward a view that still struggles for official recognition:

> It should, I think be apparent to all well-meaning people that true reconciliation between the Australian nation and its Indigenous peoples is not achievable in the absence of acknowledgment by the nation of the wrongfulness of the past dispossession, oppression and degradation of the Aboriginal peoples. That is not to say that individual Australians who had no part in what was done in the past should feel or acknowledge personal guilt. It is simply to assert our identity as a nation and the basic fact that national shame, as well as national pride, can and should exist in relation to past acts and omissions.[32]

One of the last pieces of research I undertook in uncovering the story of 'the grand experiment' was to look once more at Salvado's diary, written in a long, sloping hand, to see where Conaci and Dirimera are referred to by name. Most often they are referred to as 'the boys', 'my boys' or 'one of the native boys', leaving me to speculate about which recorded response was made by which child. As a monk who had no family of his own, Salvado had a limited understanding of Conaci and Dirimera's experiences, as he saw them less as children and more as idealised representatives of their race.

Salvado thought the Yuet people needed to be saved from their traditional beliefs and 'superstitions' if they were to survive in the new Australia. Instead, Conaci and Dirimera, by being taken out of their community and used as subjects in 'the grand experiment', were deprived of their bearings, their land, their families, their names and ultimately their childhood. The one achievement of 'the grand experiment' was that these two children became what Salvado had thought they were all along: lost souls.

⌐

As the Yuet dancing song that Salvado carefully transcribed comes towards its end, the notes rise higher and become faster. The swift pace of the song is relentless. The bass of the drum or rhythm stick, stops and the song concludes with a high F note singing out shrill, and a low F note echoing it sharply—these two sounds recalling the quick, breathless laugh of a running child.

The Lord's Prayer
in the Yuet Language

Mam n-garla yera yaka
Father up in the sky, sit down
Nunda kwella gwabba-djel
Your name is very good
Maya nunda n-garla yang-a
Your house shelters me
Nunda kwen-djel Bumbar Maman
You are the father of us all
Year-ka G-narda ka
up in the sky, while on earth
Yai maranj ngarla yang-a
today you give us food
N-garla windong nunda unyan
You forget our sins
Windong wamma n-garla unyan
We forgive the sins of others
Windji-djel n-garla windong caia
Leave us now with no evil

From the Benedictine Community of New Norcia Archive

207

Further Information

For further information about Indigenous people in Australia today and reconciliation, I would suggest you refer to the following organisations:

Australian Institute of Aboriginal and Torres Strait Islander Studies
www.aiatsis.gov.au

Australians for Native Title and Reconciliation
www.antar.org.au

European Network for Indigenous Australian Rights
www.eniar.org

Australian Human Rights and Equal Opportunity Commission
Aboriginal and Torres Strait Islander Social Justice
www.hreoc.gov.au/social_justice/index.html

Jumbunna Indigenous House of Learning
www.jumbunna.uts.edu.au

National Indigenous Times
www.nit.com.au

Reconciliation Australia
www.reconciliation.org.au

Endnotes

Note: Much of the detail of this story is drawn from E. J. Stormon's 1977 translation of Rosendo Salvado's memoirs. These notes give page references only for substantial quotes from those memoirs.

Preface

1 Reynolds, *The Other Side of the Frontier*, p. 140.
2 Hutchinson, *A Town Like No Other*, p. 5. The grave of this man, Henry Indich, was paid for by Salvado and may be seen today at the cemetery of the New Norcia monastery.
3 Historical Outline of New Norcia's Missionary Community.

Land

1 Salvado, *The Salvado Memoirs*, p. 54.
2 Ibid., p. 50.

3 Brothers' Road is left of today's Geraldton Road at Hay Flat, between New Norcia and Bindoon. It reduced travel time to Perth by 2–3 days.

4 Ibid., p. 51.

5 Russo, *Lord Abbott of the Wilderness*, p. 6.

6 Linage Conde, *Rosendo Salvado*, p. 21.

7 The full name of the monastery is Abbazia della SS. Trinità Badia di Cava de' Tirreni, or Abbazia Benedettina della SS Trinita, Cava de' Tirreni.

8 Salvado, *The Salvado Memoirs*, p. 54.

9 Ibid.

10 Ibid., p. 128.

11 Ibid., p. 55.

12 Ibid., p. 67.

13 On 10 August 1846, Fontienne started his journey back to the Benedictine Monastery of Solesmes in France, where his letters have been preserved. They reveal a man sensitive to suffering— particularly to the plight of Aboriginal prisoners chained to one another and incarcerated at Rottnest Island.

14 Salvado, *The Salvado Memoirs*, p. 69.

15 Ibid.

16 Ibid., p. 121.

17 Russo, *Lord Abbott of the Wilderness*, p. 131.

18 Salvado, *The Salvado Memoirs*, pp. 71, 78.

19 Ibid., p. 85.

20 Ibid., p. 72.

21 Ibid., p. 73.

22 Ibid., p. 76.

23 Ibid., pp. 22–4.

24 *Wollaston's Albany Journals*, p. 144.

25 During a visit by the King of the Two Sicilies to the monastery of Cava he remarked to the Abbot on the energy of Serra and Salvado: 'You are really squeezing the best out of those two Spanish lemons'. Reported in Linage Conde, *Rosendo Salvado*, p. 47.

26 Salvado, *The Salvado Memoirs*, p. 57.

27 Ibid., p. 68.

28 Ibid., p. 7.

29 Russo, *Lord Abbott of the Wilderness*, p. 33.

Endnotes

30 Ibid., p. 42.

31 Salvado, *The Salvado Memoirs*, p. 31.

32 Ibid.

33 Ibid., p. 56.

34 Ibid., p. 31.

35 Green & Tilbrook (eds), *Aborigines of New Norcia 1845–1914: The Bicentennial Dictionary of Western Australians*, p. 28.

36 Born in 1798, Madden was also known as the author of *Lives of United Irishmen*, 7 volumes, 1843–47.

Sea

1 As quoted in 'The final stretch—creating peace and reconciliation', *New Internationalist*, April 1999, p. 21.

2 Salvado, *The Salvado Memoirs*, p. 29.

3 Ibid., p. 79.

4 Ibid., p. 15.

5 Ibid., p. 90.

Africa

1 Hunt, *Cape Town Halfway to Sydney 1788–1870*.

2 van Heyningen et al., *Cape Town*, p. 160.

3 Quoted in Meltzer, The Growth of Cape Town Commerce and the Role of John Fairbairn's *Advertiser* 1835–1859, p. 133.

4 Salvado, *The Salvado Memoirs*, p. 31.

5 van Heyningen et al., *Cape Town*, p. 156.

6 Salvado, *The Salvado Memoirs*, p. 91.

7 Ibid., p. 37.

8 Ibid., p. 38.

9 Henry George Grey, or Earl Grey the Third, was the son of Charles Grey, or Earl Grey the Second, who received a gift from the East

India Company of black tea flavoured with bergamot oil, that became known as Earl Grey tea.

10　Later that year, the convict ship *Neptune* had to be sent away from the Cape, due to public protest. Transportation of convicts to New South Wales ceased a year later, and to Tasmania in 1853, after similar complaints.

11　Hunt, *Cape Town Halfway to Sydney 1788–1870.*

12　de Gruchy & de Gruchy, *The Church Struggle in South Africa*, pp. 3–11.

13　Salvado, *The Salvado Memoirs*, p. 91.

14　Bell, 'Fernando's Hideaway', p. 6.

15　Salvado, *The Salvado Memoirs*, p. 91.

Great Britain

1　Quoted in Davies 'The Industrial Revolution', pp. 176–9.

2　This is supposition, based on the fact that rail was not yet operating between the two cities, which served primarily as ports, transporting people and goods by sea.

3　Duncan, *Report on the Sanitary Condition of Liverpool*, p. 2.

4　Chadwick, 'The Sanitary Conditions of the Labouring Population'.

5　Muir, *A History of Liverpool*, p. 324

6　Ibid., p. 305.

7　*Picture of Liverpool*, 1834, as cited at
http://freepages.genealogy.rootsweb.com/~liverpool/St%20Luke.html

8　www.catholicireland.net/pages/index.php?nd=109&ant=411

9　Salvado, *The Salvado Memoirs*, p 93.

10　Dickens, *Little Dorrit*, p. 46.

11　Picard, *Victorian London*, p. 75.

12　Salvado, *The Salvado Memoirs*, p. 29.

13　www.westminister-abbey.org

14　Salvado, *The Salvado Memoirs*, p. 94.

15　Dickens, *Our Mutual Friend*, p. 147.

France

1 Stearns et al., *World History*, p. 519.
2 That Conaci rather than Dirimera asked this question is supposition, for Salvado's memoirs attribute the questioning to 'one of the native boys'.
3 Salvado, *The Salvado Memoirs*, p. 94.
4 Ibid., p. 95.
5 www.philomena.org/ULRA/jaricot2.html
6 Mogg, 'A Short History of Radical Puppetry'.
7 Stearns et al., *World History*, p. 520.
8 Salvado, *The Salvado Memoirs*, pp. 95–6.

Italy

1 Salvado, *The Salvado Memoirs*, p. 98.
2 Ibid.
3 Tomasi di Lampedusa, *The Leopard*, pp. 10–11.
4 This is supposition; in Salvado's memoirs this incident is related as 'one of the native boys'.
5 Linage Conde, *Rosendo Salvado*, p. 21.
6 Russo, *Lord Abbott of the Wilderness*, pp. 14–16.
7 Salvado, *The Salvado Memoirs*, p. 58.
8 Linage Conde, *Rosendo Salvado*, p. 22.
9 Ibid., pp 22–4.
10 Russo, *Lord Abbott of the Wilderness*, p. 19.
11 Salvado, *The Salvado Memoirs*, p. 18.
12 Ibid., p. 19.
13 Ibid.
14 Ibid., p. 20.
15 Russo, *Lord Abbott of the Wilderness*, p. 21.
16 Salvado, *The Salvado Memoirs*, p. 126.
17 Ibid., p. 122.
18 Russo, *Lord Abbott of the Wilderness*, p. 4.
19 Linage Conde, Rosendo Salvado, p. 21.

20 *Catholic Encyclopaedia* as cited at http://www.newadvent.org
21 Benedict, Saint, *The Rule of Saint Benedict*, p. 19.
22 Ibid., p. 43.
23 Ibid., p. 61.
24 Ibid.
25 Ibid.
26 Salvado, *The Salvado Memoirs*, p. 133.
27 Ibid., p. 123.
28 Benedictine Community of New Norcia Archive.
29 Salvado, *The Salvado's Memoirs*, p. 124.
30 Benedictine Community of New Norcia Archive.
31 Salvado, *The Salvado Memoirs*, p. 287.
32 This is my translation of the original letter held at St Paul's Outside the Walls Monastery Archives.
33 Benedictine Community of New Norcia Archive.
34 Russo, *Lord Abbott of the Wilderness*, p. 145.
35 Ibid., p. 146.

Coming Home

1 This translation was given to me by a monk at St Paul's Outside the Walls Monastery Archives.
2 Salvado, *The Salvado Memoirs*, pp. 39–40.
3 The original letter, in English, is held at St Paul's Outside the Walls Monastery Archives.
4 This is my translation of the original letter held at the Benedictine Community of New Norcia Archive.
5 See above.
6 O'Grady, *Corregio Jones and the Runaways*, p. 54.
7 Burial Registrations, New Norcia.
8 Ibid.
9 Russo, *Lord Abbott of the Wilderness*, p. 259.
10 Ibid., p. 2.

Findings of the Grand Experiment

1 St Paul's Outside the Walls Monastery Archives.
2 Russo, *Lord Abbott of the Wilderness*, p. 3.
3 Salvado, *The Salvado Memoirs*, p. 133.
4 Ibid., p. 63.
5 Russo, *Lord Abbott of the Wilderness*, p. 129.
6 R. M. Berndt, 'Introduction to Part 4', in Salvado, *The Salvado Memoirs*, p. 270.
7 Bates, 'Efforts Made by Western Australia Towards the Betterment of Her Aborigines', p. 1.
8 Palmieri's diary, 1853, St Paul's Outside the Walls Monastery Archives.
9 Salvado, *The Salvado Memoirs*, p. 122.
10 Marsh, 'Further Information Respecting the Aborigines'.
11 Russo, *Lord Abbott of the Wilderness*, p. 29.
12 Salvado, *The Salvado Memoirs*, p. 115.
13 Ibid., p. 118.
14 Ibid., p. 117.
15 Ibid., p. 140.
16 Bates, 'Efforts Made by Western Australia Towards the Betterment of Her Aborigines', pp. 16–17.
17 Ibid., p. 9.
18 Ibid.
19 Linage Conde, *Rosendo Salvado*, p. 20.
20 Quoted in Russo, *Lord Abbott of the Wilderness*, p. 170.
21 Bates, 'Efforts Made by Western Australia Towards the Betterment of Her Aborigines', p. 9.
22 Salvado, *The Salvado Memoirs*, pp. 118–19.
23 Ibid., p. 119.
24 Nightingale, 'Note on the Aboriginal Races in Australia', p. 7.
25 Benedictine Community of New Norcia Archive.
26 St Paul's Outside the Walls Monastery Archives.
27 Benedictine Community of New Norcia Archive.
28 *Report of the National Inquiry into the Separation of Aboriginal and Torres Strait Islander Children from Their Families*, ch. 7.
29 Benedictine Community of New Norcia Archive.

30 Hutchinson (ed.), *A Town Like No Other*, p. 63.
31 Green and Tilbrook (eds), *Aborigines of New Norcia 1845–1914*, p. xix.
32 *Report of the National Inquiry into the Separation of Aboriginal and Torres Strait Islander Children from Their Families*, 'Introduction'.

Bibliography

Bates, Daisy, 'Efforts Made by Western Australia Towards the Betterment of Her Aborigines', Government Printer, Perth, 1907.

Bell, Gavin, 'Fernando's Hideaway', *Observer*, 13 June 1999.

Benedict, Saint, *The Rule of Saint Benedict*, translated by R. J. Crotty, University of Western Australia Press, Perth, 1963.

Chadwick, Edwin, 'The Sanitary Conditions of the Labouring Population', London, 1842.

Davies, H. R. 'The Industrial Revolution', in W. Balchin (ed.), *Swansea and Its Region*, University College of Swansea, Swansea, 1971.

de Gruchy, John & Steve de Gruchy, *The Church Struggle in South Africa: 25th anniversary edition*, Fortress Press, Minneapolis, 2005.

Dickens, Charles, *Little Dorrit*, Penguin Books, Suffolk UK, 1998 [1847].

——*Our Mutual Friend*, Penguin Books, Suffolk UK, 1997 [1865].

Duncan, Dr William. *Report on the Sanitary Condition of Liverpool*, Liverpool UK, 1839.

Green, Neville & Lois Tilbrook (eds), *Aborigines of New Norcia 1845–1914: The bicentennial dictionary of Western Australians*, University of Western Australia Press, Perth, 1989.

Historical Outline of New Norcia's Missionary Community, New Norcia Monastery Archives, 2953a.

Hunt, Susan, *Cape Town Halfway to Sydney 1788–1870*, brochure, Museum of Sydney, Sydney, 2005.

Hutchinson, David (ed.), *A Town Like No Other: The living tradition of New Norcia*, Fremantle Arts Centre Press, Fremantle, 1995.

Linage Conde, Antonio, *Rosendo Salvado: Odyssey of a Galician in Australia*, Xunta de Galicia, Bilbao, 1999.

Marsh, Edward, 'Further Information Respecting the Aborigines', a presentation to the Meeting for Sufferings in Houndsditch, London, 1842.

Meltzer, J. L., The Growth of Cape Town Commerce and the Role of John Fairbairn's *Advertiser* 1835–1859, MA thesis, University of Cape Town, Cape Town, 1989.

Mogg, Kerry, 'A Short History of Radical Puppetry', *Fifth Estate Newspaper*, spring 2000.

Mudrooroo, *Aboriginal Mythology*, Thorsons, Glasgow, 1994.

Muir, Ramsay, *A History of Liverpool*, University Press of Liverpool / Williams & Norgate, London, 1907.

Nightingale, Florence, 'Note on the Aboriginal Races in Australia', Emily Faithfull, London, 1865.

O'Grady, Desmond, *Corregio Jones and the Runaways: The Italo-Australian connection*, Cardigan Street Press, Melbourne, 1995.

Picard, Liza, *Victorian London: The Life of a City 1840–1870*, Weidenfeld and Nicolson, London, 2005.

Picture of Liverpool, 1834,
http://freepages.genealogy.rootsweb.com/~liverpool/St%20Luke.html

Report of the National Inquiry into the Separation of Aboriginal and Torres Strait Islander Children from Their Families,
www.austlii.edu.au/au/special/rsproject/rslibrary/hreoc/stolen

Reynolds, Henry, *The Other Side of the Frontier: An interpretation of the Aboriginal response to the invasion and settlement of Australia*, James Cook University, Townsville, 1981.

Ride, Anouk, 'The Final Stretch, Creating peace and reconciliation', *New Internationalist*, April 1999.

Russo, George, *Lord Abbott of the Wilderness: The life and times of Bishop Salvado*, Polding Press, Melbourne, 1980.

Salvado, Rosendo, *The Salvado Memoirs: historical memoirs of Australia and particularly of the Benedictine Mission of New Norcia and of the habits and customs of the Australian natives,* translated by E. J. Stormon, University of Western Australia Press, Perth, 1977.

Stearns, Peter, Donald Schwartz & Barry Beyer, *World History: Traditions and new directions,* Addison-Wesley, Boston, 1989.

Tomasi di Lampedusa, Guiseppe, *The Leopard,* translated by Archibald Colquhoun, Harvill Press, London, 1996 [1960].

van Heyningen, Elizabeth, Nigel Worden & Vivian Bickford Smith, *Cape Town: The making of a city,* Verloren Publishers, Amsterdam, 1998.

Wollaston's Albany Journals (1848–1856): being volume 2 of the journals and diaries (1841–1856) of the Revd John Ramsden Wollaston MA, Archdeacon of Western Australia, edited by Canon A. Burton & Canon P. U. Henn, Paterson Brokensha, Perth, 1954.

Anouk Ride has worked as a journalist and editor for over ten years, contributing to magazines in Australia, the US and Europe, including the *New Internationalist*. She has a Masters in International Relations and has written on a wide range of topics from health and human rights to international politics and the environment. She lives in Melbourne. www.anoukride.com